Introduction
to the study of
THE HOLY QUR'ĀN

D0912327

Maulana Muḥammad 'Ali

Introduction to the study of
THE HOLY QUR'ĀN

Maulana Muhammad 'Ali

AUTHOR OF

an *English Translation of the Holy Qur'ān with Commentary* (with Arabic text), *The Religion of Islam, Muhammad the Prophet, Early Caliphate, Living Thoughts of the Prophet Muhammad, The Babi Movement, A Manual of Hadith* (English); *Bayan al-Qur'ān* - Urdu Translation and Commentary of the Qur'ān in three volumes, *Fadl al-Bari* Translation and Commentary of *al-Sahih al-Bukhari* (Urdu), etc.

Published in U.S.A. by

Ahmadiyya Anjuman Ishaat Islam (Lahore) U.S.A.
P.O. Box 3370, Dublin, OH 43016-0176, U.S.A.

1992

First Published 1936

The Ahmadiyya Anjuman Ishā'at Islām *(Ahmadiyya Society for the
propagation of Islām)*, based in Lahore, Pakistan, is an international Muslim body
devoted to the presentation of Islām through literary and missionary work. Since its
inception in 1914, it has produced a range of highly acclaimed, standard books on
all aspects of Islām, and has run Muslim missions in many parts of the world,
establishing the first ever Islāmic centres in England (at Woking) and Germany
(Berlin). The literature produced by the Anjuman, largely written by Maulana
Muhammad Ali, is deep research work of the highest quality, based purely on the
original sources of Islām. It has corrected many wrong notions about the religion of
Islām, and has received world wide acclaim for its authenticity, scholarship and
service of the faith.

Continuing the mission of *Ḥaḍrat* Mirza G̲h̲ulām Aḥmad, the mujaddid of the
14th century Hijra and promised messiah, the Ahmadiyya Anjuman seeks to revive
the original liberal, tolerant and rational spirit of Islām. It presents Islām as a great
spiritual force for bringing about the moral reform of mankind, and shows that this
religion has never advocated coercion, the use of physical force or the pursuit of
political power in its support.

Information, books and free literature on Islām may be obtained by contacting

Ahmadiyya Anjuman Ishaat Islam (Lahore) U.S.A.
P.O. Box 3370, Dublin, OH 43016-0176, U.S.A.

Email : aaii@aol.com
Phone : (614) 873-1030   Fax : (614) 873-1022
Website : www.muslim.org

Typsetting	Keywest Dataswitch Ltd.
Printers	Payette & Simms
	300 Arran Street
	St. Lambert, PQ
	Canada

Library of Congress card catalog number:	92-72494
ISBN:	0-913321-06-0

CONTENTS

Transliteration

Below is explained the system of transliteration of proper names and Arabic words as adopted in this book. It follows the most recent rules recognized by European Orientalists with very slight variations.

'   stands for *hamza*, sounding like *h* in *hour*, a sort of catch in voice.

'   stands for *'ain*, sounding like a strong guttural *hamza*.

a   sounds like *u* in *tub*.

ā   sounds like *a* in *father*

ai   sounds like *a* in *mat*; it represents a *fatha* before *yā*.

au   sounds between *au* in *auto* and *o* in *more*; it represents a *fatha* before *wāw*.

d   stands for *dāl*, being softer than *d*.

dz   stands for *dzād*, sounding between *d* and *z*.

gh   stands for *ghain* (soft guttural *g*).

h   sounds like *h* in *how*.

ḥ   smooth guttural aspirate, sounds like *h* but is sharper.

i   sounds as *i* in *pin*

ī   sounds as *ee* in *deep*.

ġ   sounds as *g* in *gem*.

kh   stands for *khā*, sounds like *ch* in the Scotch word *loch*.

q   stands for *qaf*, strongly articulated guttural *k*.

ṣ   stands for *sad*, strongly articulated, like *s* in *hiss*.

sh   stands for *shīn*, sounding like *sh* in *she*.

t   sounds like Italian dental, softer than *t*.

ṭ   strongly articulated palatal *t*.

th   sounds between *th* in *thing* and *s*.

u   sounds like *u* in *pull*.

ū   sounds like *oo* in *moot*.

ẓ   strongly articulated palatal *z*.

    Other letters sound as in English.

Chapter 1
The Holy Qur'ān
Section 1
Divisions and Arrangement

The name *Al-Qur'ān*, the proper name of the sacred Book of the Muslims, occurs several times in the Book itself (2:185, etc.). The word *qur'ān* is an infinitive noun from the root *qara'a* meaning, primarily, *he collected together things*, and also, *he read* or *recited*; and the Book is so called both because it is a collection of the best religious teachings, and because it is a Book that is or should be read: as a matter of fact, it is the most widely read Book in the whole world. It is plainly stated to be a revelation from the Lord of the worlds (26:192), or a revelation from God, the Mighty, the Wise (39:1, etc.), and so on. It was sent down to the Prophet Muhammad (47:2), having been revealed to his heart through the Holy Spirit (26:193, 194), in the Arabic language (44:58; 43:3). The first revelation came to the Prophet in the month of Ramadan (2:185) on the 25th or 27th night, which is known as *Lailat al-qadr* (97:1).

It is mentioned by the following additional names: *Al-Kitāb* (2:2), a writing which is complete in itself; *al-Furqān* (25:1), that which distinguishes between truth and falsehood, between right and wrong; *al-Dhikr* (15:9), the Reminder or a source of eminence and glory to mankind; *al-Mau'iẓa* (10:57), the Admonition; *al-Ḥukm* (13:37), the Judgment; *al-Ḥikma* (17:39), the Wisdom; *al-Shifā'* (10:57), that which heals; *al-Hudā* (72:13), that which guides or makes one attain the goal; *al-Tanzīl* (26:192), the Revelation; *al-Raḥma* (17:82), the Mercy; *al-Rūḥ* (42:52), the Spirit or that which gives life; *al-Khair* (3:104), the Goodness; *al-Bayān* (3:138), that

1

which explains all things; *al-Ni'ma* (93:11), the Blessing; *al-Burhān* (4:174), the clear Argument; *al-Qayyim* (18:2), the Maintainer; *al-Muhaimin* (5:48), the Guardian (of the previous revelation); *al-Nūr* (7:157), the Light; *al-Ḥaqq* (17:81), the Truth; *Ḥabl-Allāh* (3:103), the Covenant of God. In addition many qualifying epithets are applied to the Holy Book; such as *al-mubīn* (12:1), one that explains; *al-karīm* (56:77), the honoured; *al-majīd* (50:1), the glorious; *al-ḥakīm* (36:2), possessing wisdom; *'Arabiyy* (12:2), the Arabic; *al-'azīz* (41:4), the mighty; *al-mukarrama* (80:13), the honoured; *al-marfū'a* (80:14), the exalted; *al-muṭahhara* (80:14), the purified; *al-'ajab* (72:1), the wonderful; *mubārak* (6:92), blessed; *muṣaddiq* (6:92), confirming the truth of previous revelation.

Divisions

The Holy Qur'ān is divided into 114 chapters, each of which is called a *sūra* (2:23). The word *sūra* means literally *eminence* or *high degree*, and also *any step of a structure*, and in the Book itself it is applied to a chapter of the Qur'ān, either because of its eminence or because each chapter is, as it were, a distinct degree or step in the whole Book, which is thus compared to a structure. The chapters of the Holy Qur'ān are of varying length, the largest comprising fully one-twelfth of the entire Book and the smallest containing only three verses. Each chapter is, however, complete in itself and is therefore, called a *book*, and the whole of the Qur'ān is said to contain many books: "Pure pages wherein are rightly-directing books" (98:2,3). The longer chapters are divided into *rukū's* or sections, each section generally dealing with one subject, the different sections being inter-related. Again, each section contains a number of *āyas* or verses. The word *āya* means, originally, an *apparent sign* or *mark* and, in this sense, it comes to mean a *miracle* but it also signifies a *communication from God*, and is applied as such to a verse of the Holy Qur'ān as well as to a revelation or a law.

Thus the Holy Qur'ān is divided into a number of chapters of unequal length; each chapter, with the exception of the concluding 35 chapters, is divided into sections, the largest number of sections in a chapter being 40; and each section, as also each single-section chapter, is divided into a number of verses. The highest number of verses in a chapter is 286 and the smallest only three. The total number of verses in the Holy Qur'ān is 6,247, or 6,360, if we add to each chapter the common opening verse of *Bismillah*. For the purposes of recitation, the Holy Qur'ān is also divided into thirty parts of equal length, each called a *juz'*, every part being again subdivided into four parts. These divisions, however, have nothing to do with the subject-matter of the Qur'ān, neither has the division into seven *manzils* or portions, which is meant only for the completion of the recital of the Holy Qur'ān in seven days.

Revelation, collection and arrangement

The Qur'ān was revealed piecemeal (25:32) during a period of twenty-three years, the shorter chapters generally, and some of the larger ones, being revealed entire and at one time, while the revelation of the majority of the larger chapters and some of the shorter chapters extended over many years. The practice was, when a chapter was revealed in parts, that the Holy Prophet specified, under Divine guidance, the place of the verses revealed, and thus the arrangement of verses in each chapter was entirely his work. Similarly, the arrangement of the chapters was also the work of the Holy Prophet himself for, though no written manuscript was collected while he was living, the whole of the Qur'ān was committed to memory and repeated frequently by the Companions of the Holy Prophet. This would have been impossible unless there was a fixed order in which the chapters followed one another. Moreover, the division of the Holy Qur'ān into seven *manzils* is based on a direction of the Holy Prophet, and this division presupposes a known order of the chapters. It is in one of the earliest revelations that the Holy Qur'ān plainly speaks of its collection as well as its revelation as being a part of the Divine scheme:

> On Us devolves the collecting of it and the recitation of it (75:17).

The collection of the Holy Qur'ān — which means the arrangement of its verses and chapters — was, therefore, a work which was performed by the Holy Prophet himself under Divine guidance, and it is a mistake to think that either Abu Bakr or 'Uthman was the collector of the Qur'ān, though both of them did important work in connection with the dissemination of the written copies of the sacred text. Abu Bakr made the first complete written copy, by arranging the manuscripts written in the time of the Holy Prophet, in the order of the oral recitation of the Prophet's time. 'Uthman's work, on the other hand, was only the ordering of the copies to be made from the written manuscript of Abu Bakr's time and the placing of these copies in the various centres of Islamic learning, so that those who wrote the Holy Qur'ān might be able to compare their copies with the standard copy, and thus rectify errors which would otherwise ·have crept into the sacred text. The text of the Holy Qur'ān has thus been safeguarded from all alterations or corruptions in accordance with the Divine promise contained in one of the earliest revelations: "We have revealed the Reminder and We will surely be its guardian" (15:9).

Makka and Medina revelations

Another division of the Holy Book concerns the Makka and Madina revelations. Of the twenty-three years over which the revelation of the entire Book is spread thirteen years were passed by the Holy Prophet at Makka and ten were passed at Madina, to which city he had to fly for the safety of his own life and the lives of his followers. Of the entire number of chapters, ninety-three were revealed at Makka and twenty-one were revealed at Madina, but the 110th chapter, though belonging to the Madina period, was revealed at Makka during the well-known Farewell pilgrimage. The Madina chapters, being generally larger, contain really one-third of the entire Qur'ān. In arrangement, the Makka revelation is intermixed with the Madina revelation. Thus the Holy Qur'ān opens with a Makka revelation which is entitled the "Opening", and is followed by four chapters revealed at Madina, which take up over one-fifth of the whole Book. Then follow alternately Makka and Madina revelations, and the entire book is divided into the following Makka and Madina chapters following each other alternately: 1, 4, 2, 2, 14, 1, 8, 1, 13, 3, 7, 10, 48.

As regards the dates of the revelation of the various Makka chapters, it is difficult to assign a particular year to a particular chapter, except in rare cases, but broadly they may be divided into three groups; those revealed in the early Makka period, *i.e.,* during the first five years; those revealed in the middle Makka period, *i.e.,* up to the tenth year; and those revealed during the late Makka period. The dates of the Madina chapters, on the other hand, are tolerably certain and definite, but in this case the difficulty is that the revelation of the longer chapters extended over lengthy periods, and a chapter which undoubtedly belongs to the earliest days at Madina sometimes contains verses which were revealed in the closing days of the Prophet's life.

Subject to the remarks made above, the following dates may approximately be assigned to the different chapters or groups of chapters:

Early Makka period	60 Chapters:	1, 17-21, 50-56, 67-109, 111-114
Middle Makka period	17 Chapters:	29-32, 34-39, 40-46
Late Makka period	15 Chapters:	6, 7, 10-16, 22, 23, 25-28
A.H. 1-2	6 Chapters:	2, 8, 47, 61, 62, 64
A.H. 3-4	3 Chapters:	3, 58, 59
A.H. 5-8	9 Chapters:	4, 5, 24, 33, 48, 57, 60, 63, 65
A.H. 9-10	4 Chapters:	9, 49, 66, 110

The first five verses of the 96th chapter were undoubtedly the first revelation, and these were equally certainly followed by the first part of the 74th chapter, which again was, in all probability, followed by the first chapter, after which came the first part of the 73rd chapter. Beyond this, it is impossible to give a tolerably certain order. The attempt to give a chronological order is an undoubted failure, as even the shorter chapters were not revealed entire. For instance, a chronological order would place the 96th chapter first, while, as a matter fact, every historian of Islam knows that only the first five verses were revealed first, vv. 6-19 coming long afterwards, when persecution of the Prophet had actually begun (as is made clear by vv. 9, 10, which speak of the Prophet being prohibited from saying his prayers), and must be referred to about the time when Arqam's house was chosen for saying prayers, an event belonging to the fourth year of the ministry. If, then, we are confronted with such a serious difficulty in giving the first place to a chapter with which the revelation of the Holy Qur'ān undoubtedly began, what about the later chapters, and especially the longer ones? Take the second chapter in the present order as another example. There is not the least doubt that its revelation began in the first or, at the latest, in the second year of Hijra, but it is equally certain that it contains verses which were revealed in 10 A.H. A chronological order of the different chapters is, therefore, an impossibility, and all that we can say with tolerable certainty is that the greater part of a certain chapter was revealed during a certain period, and this is my reason for assigning particular periods to particular chapters.

The first thing that strikes us in the present arrangement is the intermingling of Makka and Madina revelations. Surely there must have been some reason underlying this arrangement and, to discover this, we must find the chief features, if there are any, which distinguish the Makka from the Madina revelations. A contrast of the two makes it clear that, while the Makka revelation grounded the Muslims in faith in God, the Madina revelation was meant to translate the faith into action. It is true that exhortations for good and noble deeds are met with in the Makka revelation and that faith is still shown in the Madina revelation to be the foundation on which the structure of deeds should be built, but, in the main, stress is laid in the former on faith in an Omnipresent and Omnipotent God Who requites every good and evil deed, while the latter deals chiefly with what is good and what is evil; in other words, with the details of the law. Another feature distinguishing the two revelations is that, while the Makka revelation is generally prophetical, the revelation that came down at Madina deals with the fulfilment of prophecy. Again, if the Makka revelation shows how true happiness of mind may be sought in communion with God, the Madina revelation points out how man's dealing with man may be a source of bliss and comfort to him. Hence, a scientific arrangement of the Holy Qur'ān could be made to rest only on the intermingling of the two revelations, - on the intermingling of faith with deeds, of prophecy with the fulfilment of prophecy, of Divine communion with man's relation to and treatment of man.

A cursory view of the present arrangement

A detailed view of the order in which the chapters follow one another shows the truth of the remarks made above; and for this the reader is referred to the introductory remarks prefacing each chapter in my Translation of the Holy Qur'ān. A brief outline, however, may be given here. The Holy Book is prefaced with a short Makka chapter which, in its seven short verses, contains the essence of the whole of the Qur'ān, and teaches us a prayer which is admittedly the most beautiful of all prayers taught by any religion, and which sets before us an ideal greater than any other which can be conceived. If the preface is the quintessence of the Qur'ān and places before man the highest ideal, the commencement of the Book is equally scientific, for the second chapter opens with a clear statement as to its aims and objects. The first four chapters all belong to the Madina revelation and, occupying as they do over a fifth of the whole Qur'ān, deal in detail with the teachings of Islam, comparing them with the previously existing teaching, particularly Jewish and Christian, which had by that time become the prototypes of error in religion, the former laying too much stress on outward ritual, while utterly neglecting the spirit, and the latter condemning law itself, trusting to faith in Christ alone. Almost the whole of the Islamic law dealing with the individual, home and civic life of man is contained in these four chapters.

These are followed by two of the longest Makka chapters, the first of which deals in detail with the doctrine of Divine Unity, and the second with that of prophethood. This latter chapter illustrates the doctrine of prophethood with reference to the histories of some well-known prophets. These two are again followed by two Madina chapters which fit in with the context, as they show what punishment was meted out to the opponents of the Holy Prophet; the first of these deals with their discomfiture in the first struggle in the battle of Badr and the second with their final vanquishment. Then follows a group of seven chapters, the *Alif-Lam-Ra* group, dealing with the truth of the Prophet's revelation, internal evidence, evidence from man's nature, from the histories of the previous prophets and from external nature, being produced to establish that truth. Another group of five Makka chapters follows it, all dealing with the greatness to which Islam was destined to rise, with special reference to Jewish history in ch. 17, to Christian history and doctrine in ch. 18 and ch. 19, to the history of Moses in ch. 20, and to the history of prophets in general in ch. 21. Two more Makka chapters follow, the first showing that the Prophet's cause must triumph, though the faithful would be required to make great sacrifices for the cause of truth, and the second showing that the foundation on which the greatness of the Muslim nation rested was moral, not material. A Madina chapter is then brought in to show how the prophecies of the Makka revelations were being brought to fulfilment by the establishment of a Muslim kingdom and the dissemination of the spiritual light of Islam.

The 25th chapter is again a Makka revelation, which shows, as its name indicates, that the distinction between truth and falsehood which the Holy Qur'ān was to establish was witnessed in the lives of the Companions of the Holy Prophet. A group of three more Makka chapters, the *Ta-Sin* group, is then introduced, prophesying the ultimate triumph of the Holy Prophet, with special reference to the triumph of Moses over a powerful enemy who was bent upon destroying the Israelites. Another group of four Makka chapters, the *Alif-Lam-Mim* group, follows and shows that the state of helplessness and utter weakness in which the Muslims were at the time would soon be changed. A Madina chapter is again inserted showing how the combined forces of the enemies of Islam in the battle of the Confederates failed to crush Islam. The utmost simplicity of the Holy Prophet's domestic life is then brought in to show that the attractions of this world, such as wealth or kingdom, had no charm for him (notwithstanding that he then ruled Arabia) and that thenceforward he was a model for all nations and for all ages, no prophet being needed after him, and emphasising that it was only short-sighted carpers who found fault with one who led a life of such unexampled purity and simplicity.

A group of six Makka chapters follows, showing that the rise and fall of nations are brought about by the good and evil which they do, and that nations which rise to greatness can retain their eminent position only if they are not ungrateful for the favours conferred upon them. The next group of seven Makka chapters is known as the *Ha-Mim* group, and it lays stress on the fact that truth must overcome opposition and that no temporal power with all the temporal resources at its back can annihilate truth. This is followed by a group of three Madina chapters; the 47th, which was revealed in the first years of Hijra, showing that those who had accepted the truth as revealed to the Prophet, though in great distress, would soon have their condition ameliorated; the next, which belongs to the sixth year of Hijra, predicting in the clearest words the final triumph of Islam over all the religions of the world; and the last of this group, which was revealed towards the close of the Holy Prophet's life, enjoining on the Muslims the duty of respect for one another.

From the 50th to the 56th, is another group of six Makka chapters, pointing out the great spiritual awakening which was to be brought about by the Holy Qur'ān. Then comes the last group of Madina revelations, ten chapters in all, from the 57th to the 66th, which supplement what has already been said in the previous Madina chapters, the last of these, the 65th and 66th, being clearly a supplement to the first Madina chapter, the Cow, and dealing with the subject of divorce and temporary separation. Then follow forty-eight short Makka chapters, showing how men and nations can rise to eminence by following the truth which is revealed in the Holy Qur'ān, and how they suffer loss by rejecting the truth which is revealed in it. The Holy Book ends with a concise but clear declaration of Divine Unity, in chapter 112; the last two chapters tell a man how to fly to Divine protection for refuge from all kinds of mischief.

Section 2
Interpretation

Of all the religious books of the world, the Holy Qur'ān is the only one that has laid down the rule for its own interpretation. This is contained in an early Madina chapter which deals with the Christian error of ascribing Divinity to Jesus, and runs thus:

> He it is Who has revealed the Book to thee: some of its verses are decisive, they are the basis of the Book, and others are allegorical; then as for those in whose hearts there is perversity, they follow the part of it which is allegorical seeking to mislead and seeking to give it their own interpretation; but none knows its interpretation except God, and those well-grounded in knowledge: they say, 'We believe in it, it is all from our Lord'; and none do mind except those having understanding (3:7).

We will analyse first the various statements made here. In the first place, it is stated that the Holy Qur'ān contains both kinds of verses, decisive as well as allegorical, the latter being those which are susceptible of different interpretations. We are then told that the decisive verses are the basis of the Book; *i.e.,* they contain the fundamental principles of religion, so that the allegorical statements do not in any way interfere with the basic doctrines. The next point is that some people seek to give to allegorical statements their own interpretation and thus mislead people; in other words, serious errors arise only when the fundamentals of religion are based on allegorical statements. The concluding words give a clue to the right mode of interpretation in the case of allegorical statements. The words "it is all from our Lord" signify that there is no disagreement between the various portions of the Holy Book. This principle is followed by those who are well-grounded in knowledge; *i.e.,* the rule of interpretation which they follow is to refer passages which are susceptible of various interpretations to those whose meaning is obvious, and to subject particular statements to general principles.

The Qur'ān establishes in clear words certain principles which are to be taken as the basis, while there are other statements which are either made in allegorical words or are susceptible of different meanings, the interpretation of which must be in consonance with the fundamental principles which are laid down in clear and decisive words. In fact, this is true of every writing. When a certain law is laid down in a book in unmistakable words, any statement carrying a doubtful significance, or one which is apparently opposed to the law so laid down, must be interpreted subject to the principle enunciated.

The subject is very appropriately dealt with as a prelude to a controversy with the Christians, who attribute Divinity to Jesus and uphold the doctrine of atonement by blood on the basis of certain ambiguous words or allegorical statements contained in prophecies, without heeding the fundamental principles laid down in books which they themselves accept as revealed by God. The Unity of God is so clearly laid down as the basis of the religion of all prophets in the Old Testament that, if the allegorical nature of certain prophecies had been kept in mind, the blunder of Church Christianity, the Divinity of Christ, would have been impossible. This gravest mistake in human history was made only by disregarding the right principle of interpretation. The metaphorical language of the prophecies was made the basis of Christianity, and the doctrines of Divinity of Christ, Atonement and Trinity followed and were formulated gradually as the basic doctrines of the Christian faith.

The epithet "son of God" was freely used in Israelite literature, and was always taken allegorically. The term occurs as early as Gen. 6:2 where the "sons of God" are spoken of as taking daughters of men for wives. It occurs again in Job 1:6 and 38:7, and *good men* are no doubt meant in both places. In Ex. 4:22 and many other places, the Israelites are spoken of as the children of God: "Israel is my son, even my first-born." The expression is used in the same metaphorical sense in the Gospels. Even in John, where the Divinity of Christ is looked upon as finding a bolder expression than in the synoptics,

Jesus Christ is reported as saying in answer to those who accused him of blasphemy for speaking of himself as the son of God:

> Is it not written in your law, I said, ye are gods? If he called them gods, unto whom the word of God came and the scripture cannot be broken, say ye of him whom the Father hath sanctified, and sent into the world. Thou blasphemest, because I said, I am the son of God (John 10:34-36).

It is thus clear that, even in the mouth of Jesus, the term "son of God" was a metaphorical expression and, by taking it literally, the Church has destroyed the very foundations of religion. It is to this fundamental mistake of Christianity that the Holy Qur'ān refers by giving the rule of interpretation of allegorical verses in a discussion of the Christian religion.

For a right understanding of the Qur'ān, therefore, it is necessary to read it as a whole, to compare one part with another, and to seek the explanation of one passage by referring to another. The following rules may therefore be laid down:

1. The principles of Islam are enunciated in decisive words in the Holy Qur'ān and therefore no attempt should be made to establish a principle on the strength of allegorical passages or of words susceptible of different meanings.

2. The explanation of the Qur'ān should in the first place be sought in the Qur'ān itself, for whatever the Qur'ān has stated briefly, or merely hinted at, in one place, will be found expanded and fully explained elsewhere in the Holy Book itself.

3. It is very important to remember that the Holy Qur'ān contains allegory and metaphor along with what is plain and decisive, and the only safeguard against being misled by what is allegorical or metaphorical is that the interpretation of such passages must be strictly in consonance with what is laid down in clear and decisive words, and not at variance therewith.

4. When a law or principle is laid down in clear words, any statement carrying a doubtful significance, or a statement apparently opposed to the law so laid down, must be interpreted subject to the

principle enunciated. Similarly, that which is particular must be read in connection with and subject to more general statements.

Section 3
The Theory of Abrogation

That certain verses of the Holy Qur'ān are abrogated by others
is now an exploded theory. The two passages on which it was
supposed to rest refer, really, to the abrogation, not of the passages
of the Holy Qur'ān, but of the previous revelations whose place the
Holy Qur'ān has taken. The first verse is contained in the chapter *al-
Naḥl* — a Makka revelation — and runs thus:

> And when We change one message for another message,[1]
> and Allah knows best what He reveals, they say, Thou art
> only a forger (16:101).

Now it is a fact admitted on all hands that details of the Islamic law
were revealed at Medina, and it is in relation to these details that the
theory of abrogation has been broached. Therefore a Makka
revelation would not speak of abrogation. But the reference in the
above verse is to the abrogation, not of the Quranic verses, but of the
previous Divine messages or revelations, involved by the revelation
of the Holy Qur'ān. The context shows this clearly to be the case, for
the opponents are here made to say that the Prophet was a forger.
Now the opponents called the Prophet a forger, not because he
announced the abrogation of certain verses of the Holy Qur'ān, but
because he claimed that the Holy Qur'ān was a Divine revelation
which had taken the place of previous revelations. Their contention
was that the Qur'ān was not a revelation at all: "Only a mortal
teaches him" (16:103). Thus they called the whole of the Qur'ān a

---

1. The word *āya* occurring here means originally *a sign*, and hence it comes to
    signify *an indication* or *evidence* or *proof*, and is used in the sense of a *miracle*.
    It also signifies *risala* or *a Divine message*. The word is frequently used in the
    Holy Qur'ān in it's general sense of a Divine message or a Divine
    communication, and is, therefore, applicable to a portion of the Holy Qur'an
    or to any previous revelation. It carries the latter significance here as the
    context clearly shows.

forgery and not merely a particular verse of it. The theory of abrogation, therefore, cannot be based on this verse which speaks only of one revelation or one law taking the place of another.

The other verse which is supposed to lend support to the theory is 2:106:

> Whatever communication We abrogate or cause to be forgotten, We bring one better than it or one like it[2].

A reference to the context will show that the Jews or the followers of previous revelations are here addressed. Of these it is said again and again:

> We believe in that which was revealed to us; and they deny what is besides that (2:91).

So they were told that if one revelation was abrogated, it was only to give place to a better. And there is mention not only of abrogation but also of something that was forgotten. Now the words "or cause to be forgotten" cannot refer to the Holy Qur'ān at all, because no portion of the Holy Book could be said to have been forgotten so as to require a new revelation in its place. There is no point in supposing that God should first make the Holy Prophet forget a verse and then reveal a new one in its place. Why not, if he really had forgotten a verse, remind him of the one forgotten? But even if we suppose that his memory ever failed in retaining a certain verse (which really never happened), that verse was quite safely preserved in writing, and the mere failure of the memory could not necessitate a new revelation. That the Prophet never forgot what was recited to him by the Holy Spirit is plainly stated in the Holy Qur'ān:

> We shall make thee recite, so thou shalt not forget (87:6).

---

2. Sale's translation of the words is misleading and has actually deceived many writers on Islam who had no access to the original. He translates the words *nunsi-ha* as meaning *we cause thee to forget*. Now the text does not contain any word meaning *thee*. The slight error makes the verse mean that Almighty God had caused the Holy Prophet to forget certain Quranic verses; whereas the original does not say that the Prophet was made to forget anything but clearly implies that the world was made to forget.

History also bears out the fact that he never forgot any portion of the Quranic revelation. Sometimes the whole of a very long chapter would be revealed to him in one portion, as in the case of the sixth chapter which extends over twenty sections, but he would cause it to be written down without delay, and make his Companions learn it by heart, and recite it in public prayers, and that without the change of even a letter; notwithstanding the fact that he himself could not read from a written copy; nor did the written copies, as a rule, remain in his possession. It was a miracle indeed that he never forgot any portion of the Qur'ān, though other things he might forget, and it is to his forgetfulness in other things that the words 'except what Allah pleases' (87:7) refer. On the other hand, it is a fact that parts of the older revelation had been utterly lost and forgotten, and thus the Holy Qur'ān was needed to take the place of that which was abrogated, and that which had been forgotten by the world.

"The hadith speaking of abrogation are all weak," says Tabrasi. But it is stranger still that the theory of abrogation has been accepted by writer after writer without ever thinking that not a single hadith, however weak, touching on the abrogation of a verse, was traceable to the Holy Prophet. It never occurred to the upholders of this theory that the Quranic verses were promulgated by the Holy Prophet, and that it was he whose authority was necessary for the abrogation of any Quranic verse; no Companion, not even Abu Bakr or 'Ali, could say that a Quranic verse was abrogated. The Holy Prophet alone was entitled to say so, and there is not a single hadith to the effect that he ever said so; it is always some Companion or a later authority to whom such views are to be traced. In most cases where a report is traceable to one Companion who held a certain verse to have been abrogated, there is another report traceable to another Companion to the effect that that verse was not abrogated.[3] It shows clearly that the opinion of one Companion as to the abrogation of a verse would be

---

3. Some examples may be noted here. 2:180 is held by some to have been abrogated while others have denied it; 2:184 is considered by Ibn 'Umar as having been abrogated while Ibn 'Abbas says it was not; 2:240 was abrogated according to Ibn Zubair while Mujahid says it was not. I have taken these examples only from the second chapter of the Holy Qur'ān.

questioned by another Companion. Even among later writers we find that there is not a single verse on which the verdict of abrogation has been passed by one without being questioned by another; and while there are writers who would lightly pass the verdict of abrogation on hundreds of verses, there are others who consider not more than five to be abrogated, and even in the case of these five the verdict of abrogation has been seriously impugned by earlier writers.

The theory of abrogation has in fact arisen from a misconception of the use of the word *naskh* by the Companions of the Holy Prophet. When the significance of one verse was limited by another, it was sometimes spoken of as having been abrogated (*nusikhat*) by that other. Similarly when the words of a verse gave rise to a misconception, and a later revelation cleared up that misconception, the word *naskh* was metaphorically used in connection with it, the idea underlying its use being, not that the first verse was abrogated, but that a certain conception to which it had given rise was abrogated[4]. Earlier authorities admit this use of the word: "Those

---

4. Many instances of this may be quoted. In 2:284, it is said: "Whether you manifest what is in your minds or hide it, Allah will call you to account for it;" while according to 2:286, "Allah does not impose on any soul a duty but to the extent of its ability". A report in Bukhari says that one of the Companions of the Holy Prophet, probably 'Abd-Allah ibn 'Umar, held the opinion that the first verse was abrogated (*nusikhat*) by the second. What was meant by *naskh* (abrogation) in this case is made clear by another detailed report given in the Musnad of Ahmad. According to this report when 2:284 was revealed, "the Companions entertained an idea which they had never entertained before (or according to another report, they were greatly grieved) and thought that they had not the power to bear it. The matter being brought to the notice of the Holy Prophet, he said: 'Rather say, We have heard and we obey and submit', and so God inspired faith in their hearts." As this report shows, what happened was this, that some Companion or Companions thought that 2:284 imposed a new burden on them, making every evil idea which entered the mind without taking root or ever being translated into action, punishable in the same manner as if it had been translated into action. 2:286 made it plain that this was not the meaning conveyed by 2:284, since according to that verse, God did not impose on man a burden which he could not bear. This removal of a misconception was called abrogation (*naskh*) by Ibn 'Umar.

It may be added that there is nothing to show that 2:286 was revealed later than 2:284. On the other hand, the use of the words *we have heard and we obey* by the Holy Prophet to remove the wrong notion which some Companions

(continued...)

who accept *naskh* (abrogation) here (2:109) take it as meaning
explanation metaphorically" and again: "By *naskh* is meant
metaphorically, explaining and making clear the significance". It is
an abrogation but not an abrogation of the words of the Holy Qur'ān;
rather it is the abrogation of a misconception of their meaning. This
is further made clear by the application of *naskh* to verses containing
statement of facts (*akhbār*), whereas, properly speaking, abrogation
could only take place in the case of verses containing a
commandment or a prohibition (*amr* or *nahy*). In the ordinary sense
of the word there could be no *naskh* (abrogation) of a statement made
in the Word of God, as that would suggest that God had made a
wrong statement first and then recalled it. This use of the word *naskh*
by the earlier authorities regarding statements[5] shows that they were
using the word to signify the removal of a wrong conception

4.(...continued)

entertained - these very words occur in 2:285 - shows that the three verses, 284,
285 and 286, were all revealed together, and hence the abrogation, in the
ordinary sense of the word, of one of them by another is meaningless. There
are other instances in which a verse revealed later is thought to have been
abrogated by a previous verse. But how could a later verse be abrogated by a
previous one? Or what point can there be in giving an order which was
cancelled before it was given? If, on the other hand, the word *naskh* is taken to
mean the placing of a limitation upon the meaning of a verse, or the removal
of a wrong conception attached to it, no difficulty would arise, for even a
previous verse may be spoken of as placing a limitation upon the meaning of
a later verse or as removing a wrong conception arising therefrom.

5.   One example of one statement being spoken of as abrogated by another is that
of 2:284, 286 (for which see the previous foot-note). Another is furnished by
8:65, 66, where the first verse states that in war the Muslims shall overcome
ten times their numbers, and the second, after referring to their weakness at the
time - which meant the paucity of trained men among them and their lack of
the implements and necessaries of war - states that they shall overcome double
their numbers. Now the two verses relate to two different conditions and they
may be said to place a limitation upon the meaning of each other, but one of
them cannot be spoken of as abrogating the other. In the time of the Holy
Prophet when the Muslims were weak, when ever man, old or young, had to
be called upon to take the field, and the Muslim army was but ill-equipped, the
Muslims overcame double, even thrice, their numbers; but in the wars with the
Persian and Roman empires, they vanquished ten times their numbers. Both
statements were true; they only related to different circumstances and the one
placed a limitation upon the meaning of the other, but neither of them actually
abrogated the other.

regarding, or the placing of a limitation upon, the meaning of a certain verse. At the same time, it is true that the use of the word *naskh* soon became indiscriminate, and when any one found himself unable to reconcile two verses, he would declare one of them to be abrogated by the other.

The principle on which the theory of abrogation is based is unacceptable, being contrary to the plain teachings of the Holy Qur'ān. A verse is considered to be abrogated by another when the two cannot be reconciled with each other; in other words, when they appear to contradict each other. But the Holy Qur'ān destroys this foundation when it declares in plain words that no part of the Holy Book is at variance with another:

> Do they not then meditate on the Qur'ān, and if it were from any other than Allah, they would have found in it many a discrepancy (4:82).

It was due to lack of meditation that one verse was thought to be at variance with another; and hence it is that in almost all cases, where abrogation has been upheld by one person, there has been another who being able to reconcile the two, has repudiated the alleged abrogation.

It is only among the later commentators that we meet with the tendency to augment the number of verses thought to have been abrogated, and by some of these the figure has been placed as high as five hundred. Speaking of such Sayuti says in the *Itqān*:

> Those who multiply (the number of abrogated verses) have included many kinds — one kind being that in which there is neither abrogation nor any particularization (of a general statement), nor has it any connection with any one of them, for various reasons. And this is as in the word of God: 'And spend out of what We have given them' (2:3); 'And spend out of what We have given you' (63:10); and the like. It is said that these are abrogated by the verse dealing with Zakat, while it is not so, they being still in force.

Sayuti himself brings the number of verses which he thinks to be abrogated down to twenty-one, in some of which he considers there is abrogation, while in others he finds that it is only the particularization of a general injunction that is effected by a later verse; but he admits that there is a difference of opinion even about these.

A later writer, however, the famous Shah Wali Allah of India, commenting on this in his *Fauz al-Kabīr* says that abrogation cannot be proved in the case of sixteen out of Sayuti's twenty-one verses, but in the case of the remaining five he is of opinion that the verdict of abrogation is final. These five verses are dealt with below:

(1) 2:180: "Bequest is prescribed for you when death approaches one of you, if he leaves behind wealth for parents and near relations, according to usage". As a matter of fact, both Baidzawi and Ibn Jarir quote authorities who state that this verse was not abrogated; and it is surprising that it is considered as being abrogated by 4:11, 12, which speak of the shares to be given "after the payment of a bequest he may have bequeathed or a debt," showing clearly that the bequest spoken of in 2:180 was still in force. This verse in fact speaks of bequest for charitable objects which is even now recognized by Muslims to the extent of one third of property.

(2) 2:240: "And those of you who die and leave wives behind, (making) a bequest in favour of their wives of maintenance for a year without turning them out". But we have the word of no less an authority than Mujahid that this verse is not abrogated: "Allah gave her (*i.e.* the widow) the whole of a year, seven months and twenty days being optional, under the bequest; if she desired she could stay according to the bequest (*i.e.* having maintenance and residence for a year), and if she desired she could leave the house (and remarry), as the Qur'ān says: 'Then if they leave of their own accord, there is no blame on you'". This verse, therefore, does not contradict verse 234. Moreover, there is proof that it was revealed after verse 234 and hence it cannot be said to have been abrogated by that verse.

(3) 8:65: "If there are twenty patient ones of you, they shall overcome two hundred, etc." This is said to have been abrogated by the verse that follows it: "For the present Allah has made light your burden and He knows that there is weakness in you, so if there are a

hundred patient ones of you, they shall overcome two hundred." That the question of abrogation does not arise here at all is apparent from the words of the second verse which clearly refers to the early times when the Muslims were weak, having neither munitions of war nor experience of warfare, and when old and young had to go out and fight; while the first verse refers to a later period when the Muslim armies were fully organized and equipped.

(4) 33:52: "It is not allowed to thee to take women after this." This is said to have been abrogated by a verse which was apparently revealed before it: "O Prophet! We have made lawful to thee thy wives" (33:50). The whole issue has been turned topsy-turvy. As I have said before, a verse cannot be abrogated by one revealed before it. Apparently what happened was this. When 4:3 was revealed, limiting the number of wives to four, should exceptional circumstances require, the Prophet was told not to divorce the excess number, and this was effected by 33:50 as quoted above; but at the same time he was told not to take any woman in marriage after that, and this was done by 33:52.

(5) 58:12: "O you who believe! when you consult the Apostle, then offer something in charity before your consultation; that is better for you and purer; but if you do not find, then surely Allah is Forgiving, Merciful". This is said to have been abrogated by the verse that follows: "Do you fear that you will not be able to give in charity before your consultation? So when you do not do it, and Allah has turned to you mercifully, then keep up prayer and pay the poor-rate". It is not easy to see how one of these injunctions is abrogated by the other, since there is not the slightest difference in what they say. The second verse merely gives further explanation to show that the injunction is only in the nature of a recommendation, that is to say, a man may give in charity whatever he can easily spare, zakat (or the legal alms) being the only obligatory charity.

Thus the theory of abrogation falls to the ground on all considerations.

Section 4
Relation to Sunna

The Holy Qur'ān is the fountain-head from which all the teachings of Islam are drawn, and it is the only absolute and final authority in all discussions relating to the religion of Islam. The *Sunna*, meaning *mode of life*, and specially *the course of the Holy Prophet's life*, is used in the religious terminology of Islam to indicate *practices and sayings of the Holy Prophet. Ḥadīth*, which means originally *news*, carries the same significance. The Sunna, or Hadith, as signifying the precept and example of the Holy Prophet, is a secondary source of the law of Islam. The true relation of the Qur'ān and the Sunna has often been misunderstood, and that not only by non-Muslim critics, but even by some sections of the Muslim community, there being a tendency in some quarters to attach over-importance to the Sunna and in others to discredit it altogether. The truth lies midway between these two extremes.

In what relation does the Sunna stand to the Qur'ān? According to the Qur'ān itself, the Holy Prophet was not only the recipient of the Divine revelation, but he was also required, in one of the earliest revelations, to collect and arrange it and give explanation of it:

> On Us devolves the collecting of it and the reciting of it. So when We have recited it, follow its recitation. Again on Us devolves the explaining of it (75:17-19).

The Prophet's work to be carried out under Divine guidance was thus threefold, *viz.*, the recitation of the Qur'ān, the collection of the Qur'ān, and the explaining of the Qur'ān. He carried out the first part of his work, by reciting the Qur'ān to those around him, as it was revealed in portions; the second part, by having every portion written down as it was revealed and by assigning to the different verses and chapters as they were revealed their proper place in the Book; and the third part, by giving explanation where it was needed. This third part of his work is Sunna, or Hadith. It was an interpretation of some portions of the Qur'ān which needed explanation, given sometimes by example and sometimes by words.

In the verses quoted above, such explanation is spoken of as proceeding from a Divine source, but evidently it was not a revelation in words as was the Qur'ān, being conveyed sometimes by deeds and sometimes by words; nevertheless that explanation proceeded from a Divine source, just as the arrangement of the Qur'ān was accomplished under Divine guidance. In both cases, there was no *waḥy matluww*, a revelation recited in words, but the Prophet acted or spoke under the influence of the Divine spirit, being guided by what is called *waḥy khafi*, lit., inner revelation. Sunna, or Hadith, is, therefore, an explanation of the Qur'ān given under Divine inspiration.

Moreover, such explanation was needed. The Holy Qur'ān had given quite a new conception of religion. Religion was no longer a name for certain beliefs or certain forms of worship; it was a code for the entire life of man, and directions were, therefore, needed for man's everyday life. For various reasons, all these details could not find a place in the Holy Qur'ān and, therefore, while the Holy Qur'ān laid down the broad principles of life, the details were given by the Holy Prophet, the Holy Qur'ān touching on them in only a very few important cases. Again, the injunctions contained in the Holy Qur'ān needed illustration to show how these were to be carried into practice, and the Holy Prophet was the great exemplar whose life furnished this illustration: "Surely you have in the Apostle of God an excellent exemplar" (33:21). Thus both the words and the deeds of the Founder of Islam form a secondary source of the teachings of Islam. It was to draw attention to this that the Holy Qur'ān repeatedly enjoined the Muslims to "obey God and the Apostle" (3:132; 4:59, 69; 24:54, etc.). The fact was that the principles of religion, having been made clear and established, the Muslims still needed to be told that they had to take the details of the law from the Holy Prophet; hence the injunction to obey God and the Apostle.

Thus there is not the least doubt that Sunna, or Hadith, was, from the beginning, looked upon as a secondary source of the Islamic

teachings, and, for that reason, many of the companions of the Holy
Prophet began to preserve his sayings, mostly in memory but
sometimes also in writing. The latter course was not, however,
generally adopted, as the Prophet himself had given a warning
against it, lest by the less wary, the Quranic revelation should be
mixed up with the Sunna. However, those nearest him knew well the
value of the Sunna. Thus, as Tirmidhi and Abu Dawud relate, when
Mu'adh ibn Jabal was appointed Governor of Yemen, the Holy
Prophet asked him how he would judge cases. "By the Book of
God", was the reply. "But if you do not find it in the Book of God?",
asked the Prophet. "By the Sunna of the Apostle of God", said the
Governor-designate.

It is a mistake to suppose that the Sunna was collected two
hundred years after the Holy Prophet. Schools for the preservation
and teaching of Hadith were established immediately after his death,
and to these schools flocked students from different quarters, some
of them committing to memory the hadith which were taught there,
while others preserved them in writing. The number of these schools
soon increased, as other centres of Islamic learning and civilization
sprang up, and the later written collections of Bukhari and others
were based on these. Though it cannot be denied that the Sunna was
not preserved intact as was the Qur'ān, yet the labours of the later
collectors were so thorough that the hadith which have been handed
down to us through their searching enquiry give us a tolerably
reliable collection of Hadith. Especially in the case of hadith relating
to practice, it may be said that they furnish a reliable source of the
teachings of Islam. The collectors themselves were not as stringent
in the case of other hadith, such as those relating to stories of the
past, but these do not play any important part in our knowledge of
the teachings of Islam. As to the errors which, notwithstanding all the
precautions of the narrators and the collectors, have crept into the
hadith, there is ample scope for their rectification by means of the
Holy Qur'ān, as the Holy Prophet himself is reported to have said:

> There will be narrators reporting hadith from me, so judge
> by the Qur'ān; if a report agrees with the Qur'ān, accept it;
> otherwise reject it (Ibn 'Asakar).

Thus, notwithstanding many minor details of religious law that are taken from the Sunna, the Holy Qur'ān remains the real and the only absolute authority for the teachings of Islam, and Hadith is accepted only subject to the condition that it does not contradict the Holy Qur'ān. Even the hadith contained in the most reliable collections, the *Bukhari* and the *Muslim*, can be accepted subject to this condition.

Section 5
Relation to Earlier Scriptures

The Holy Qur'ān requires a belief not only in its own truth but also in the truth of previous scriptures delivered to prophets of the different nations of the world. At its commencement, it lays down clearly:

> And those who believe in that which has been revealed to thee and that which was revealed before thee (2:4).

The universality of what was revealed before is clearly accepted:

> And there is not a people but a warner has gone among them (35:24);

> And every nation had an apostle (10:47).

Lest any one should be misled by the names of a few of the prophets mentioned in the Holy Qur'ān, it is stated:

> And certainly We sent apostles before thee: there are some of them that We have mentioned to thee and there are others whom We have not mentioned to thee (40:78; 4:164).

Thus the Holy Qur'ān accepts the truth of the sacred books of the world, and hence it is, again and again, spoken of as a Book verifying what was before it. The basis of the relation in which the Holy Qur'ān stands to other scriptures is, therefore, that they are all members of one family; they have all a Divine origin.

The Verifier of the sacred books of the world, however, occupies a unique position among them. The relation in which the Holy Qur'ān stands to earlier scriptures is thus lucidly set forth by the Holy Book itself:

> And We have revealed to thee the Book with the truth verifying what is before it of the book and a guardian over it (5:48).

The Qur'ān is thus not only a verifier of the sacred books of all nations as stated above; it is also a guardian over them. In other words, it guards the original teachings of the prophets of God, for, as elsewhere stated, those teachings had undergone alterations, and only a revelation from God could separate the pure Divine teaching from the mass of error which had grown around it. This was the work done by the Holy Qur'ān, and hence it is called a guardian over the earlier scriptures. Of all the scriptures, it has particularly chosen the Gospels to show in what ways erroneous doctrines had almost entirely suppressed the truth preached by a prophet of God. The erroneous doctrines of Christianity were especially pointed out and stressed because the Omniscient God knew that the world would be misled more by them than by any other erroneous teaching. They seem, moreover, to have been chosen as an example, for how could earlier scriptures escape alterations if the teachings of so recent a prophet as Jesus Christ could not be handed over intact to posterity?

The Holy Qur'ān further claims that it came as a judge to decide the differences between the various religions:

> Certainly We sent apostles to nations before thee ... And We have not revealed to thee the Book except that thou mayest make clear to them that about which they differ (16:63, 64).

As already stated, the Qur'ān proclaimed that prophets had been raised in every nation, and, therefore, that every nation had received guidance from God, yet nation differed from nation even in the essentials of faith. The position of the Holy Qur'ān was, therefore, essentially that of a judge deciding between these various claimants.

The most important point to be borne in mind in connection with the relation of the Holy Qur'ān to the earlier scriptures is that it makes clear what is obscure in them and explains fully what is there stated briefly. Revelation, according to the Holy Qur'ān, is not only universal but also progressive, and it attains perfection in that final revelation. A revelation was granted to each nation according to its requirements, and in each age, in accordance with the capacity of the people of that age. As the human brain became more and more developed, more and more light was cast by revelation on matters

relating to the unseen, on the existence and attributes of the Divine
Being, on the nature of revelation from Him, on the requital of good
and evil, on the life after death, and on paradise and hell. It is for this
reason that the Holy Qur'ān is again and again called a book "that
makes manifest". It shed complete light on the essentials of the faith
and made manifest what had hitherto of necessity remained obscure.

Further, as a result of what has been said above, the Holy Qur'ān
claims that it came as a perfect revelation of Divine will:

> This day have I perfected for you your religion and
> completed My favour on you and chosen for you Islam as a
> religion (5:3).

The finality of the Quranic revelation is, therefore, based on its
perfection. New scriptures were revealed as long as they were
needed, but when perfect light was cast on all essentials of religion
in the Holy Qur'ān, no prophet was needed after him. Six hundred
years before him, Jesus Christ, who was the last among the national
prophets - the Holy Prophet Muhammad being the prophet not of one
nation but of the whole world - had declared in plain words that he
could not guide the world to perfect truth, because the world at that
stage was not in a fit condition to receive that truth: "I have yet many
things to say unto you, but ye cannot bear them now. Howbeit, when
he the spirit of truth is come, he will guide you unto all truth" (John
16:12, 13). Among the Scriptures of the world, the Holy Qur'ān,
therefore, occupies a unique position as a perfect revelation of the
Divine will.

The idea that the Qur'ān has merely borrowed something from
the earlier scriptures, especially from the Torah and the Gospels,
must be examined in the light of facts. That the Qur'ān deals with the
religious topics which are dealt with in those books goes without
saying; that it relates the history of some of the prophets whose
history is also related in the Bible is also a fact, but to say that it
borrows from those books is entirely wrong. Take first the essentials
of religion as they are dealt with in the Holy Qur'ān, and for this I
would refer the reader to the second part of the Introduction. Neither
the old nor the New Testament, nor any other sacred book, makes

any approach to the grand and noble truths that find expression in the Holy Qur'ān. Take next the histories of the prophets, as they are narrated in the Bible and as they are narrated in the Holy Qur'ān, and you will find that the latter corrects the errors of the former as it does in the matter of religious doctrines. Anyone who refers to the summary of these histories, as related further on, will see for himself the truth of these remarks. I will, however, refer here to one point in particular. The Bible speaks of many of the prophets of God as committing the most heinous sins; it speaks of Abraham as telling lies and casting away Hajar and her son; it speaks of Lot as committing incest with his own daughters; it speaks of Aaron as making a calf for worship and leading the Israelites to its worship; it speaks of David as committing adultery with Uriah's wife; it speaks of Solomon as worshipping idols; but the Holy Qur'ān accepts none of these statements, definitely rejects most of them and clears these prophets of the false charges against them. The unlearned Prophet of Arabia who had never read the Bible could not do it. It was undoubtedly the work of Divine revelation; it was surely information coming from a higher source.

Section 6
Miraculous Nature

The Holy Qur'ān claims to be the greatest miracle which was vouchsafed to a prophet. It is a miracle the like of which could not be produced even if all men should combine together. This claim to uniqueness was not an after-thought on the Prophet's part. It was consistently advanced from first to last as an argument of its Divine origin. As early as the fifth year of the Prophet's mission, when there was no sign of the Qur'ān finding acceptance in Arabia, to say nothing of the whole world, the claim to uniqueness was put forward in the clearest words:

> If men and jinn should combine together to produce the like of this Qur'ān, they could not produce the like of it though some of them were aiders of others (17:88).

Towards the close of the Makka period, when the people had shown themselves to be deaf to all appeals, the same claim was advanced again, reducing the demand to the production of ten chapters like those of the Holy Qur'ān:

> Or do they say, he has forged it? Say, then bring ten forged chapters like it, and call upon whom you can besides God, if you are truthful (11:13).

This was soon followed by the still more forcible claim that human effort could not produce even a single chapter like it:

> Or, do they say, he has forged it? Say, then bring a chapter like this and invite whom you can besides God, if you are truthful (10:38).

After the flight to Madina, when the Holy Prophet came into contact with the Jews who had the books of the prophets with them, the claim to the uniqueness of the Qur'ān was still repeated in the same forcible words:

And if you are in doubt as to that which We have revealed
to Our servant, then produce a chapter like it, and call on
your helpers besides God, if you are truthful (2:23).

The golden days of Arabic poetry were those which immediately
preceded the time of the Holy Prophet, yet history bears clear
testimony to the fact that the Arabs never attempted to dispute the
claim of the Holy Qur'ān. Why? Did they not consider this matter
sufficiently serious? They no doubt looked upon the Prophet at first
as a mere visionary and then as a poet, but they soon began to realize
the serious situation. Three or four years of work had brought to the
Prophet's banner a band of over one hundred devoted followers who,
rather than give up their faith in him, had shown their readiness to
suffer every torture and every privation, who had left their very
country to take shelter in a neighbouring land. The opponents of
Islam had taken the matter so seriously that, unable to seize the
flying Muslims in their pursuit of them, they sent a deputation to
persuade the Negus to hand over to them their kinsmen. They had
seen how deep-rooted was faith in the hearts of those who had
accepted the life-giving message of the Qur'ān; they had tried all
means to put a stop to the activities of the Prophet; they had
persecuted him and his followers; they had put as much pressure as
they could on Abu Talib, the Prophet's uncle, to hand him over to
them; they had sent deputation after deputation to dissuade the
Prophet from speaking against their ancestral religion; and, therefore,
if they could silence the Prophet by accepting his challenge to
produce a chapter like the Holy Qur'ān, they would surely have done
it. Being harassed with the question again and again, they made the
empty boast that, if they pleased, they could say the like of it, as it
contained nothing but stories of the ancients (8:31); but they knew
well that stories could not bring about the transformation which the
Qur'ān was working in the lives of a dead nation, and hence they
never made a serious attempt to bring forward anything to answer the
challenge of the Qur'ān.

The great gift which the Qur'ān claimed from first to last as its
special privilege was guidance, the purifying of man from the
pollution of sin, and making him fulfil the purpose of life by the

development of the faculties with which he was endowed. It opens
with the statement that the Qur'ān offers guidance to humanity to
reach the great goal of life:

> This Book, there is no doubt of it, is a guidance to those who
> guard against evil (2:2).

Its purifying power was so great that those who accepted the message
had their lives entirely transformed. Moreover, its convincing power
was simply irresistible. The Arabs had strongly resisted long-
sustained and influential Jewish and Christian efforts to give up their
idolatry and superstitions, and monotheism had never appealed to
them as a nation; but the message of the Qur'ān, notwithstanding all
the efforts of the leaders to dissuade people from listening to it and
with all their scoffing and jeering at it, made quite a different
impression. It touched their very souls though, for the sake of their
national honour, they would not accept it. When the 53rd chapter,
which ends with a commandment to prostrate oneself, was recited by
the Holy Prophet in an assembly containing Muslims as well as
idolaters, even the latter fell down in prostration, with the single
exception of Umayya ibn Khalf, who raised some gravel to his
forehead. When Abu Bakr recited the Qur'ān aloud in the courtyard
of his house, which was situated on a public way, the idolaters
objected and sanctioned Abu Bakr's staying at Makka only on
condition that he would not recite the Qur'ān aloud, because, they
said, women and children were carried away by it. On another
occasion, when 'Utba ibn Rabi'a came to the Holy Prophet with a
message from the Quraish that, if he desisted from speaking of their
national gods, they were prepared to accept him as their chief and to
offer what he desired, the Holy Prophet read out to him the opening
verses of the 41st chapter. He was so impressed with the words and
was such a changed man when he went back to the Quraish leaders
and asked them not to oppose the Prophet, for what he had heard
from him was neither poetry, nor magic, nor a soothsayer's utterance,
that his friends had to tell him that he was under the magic spell of
Muhammad. 'Umar went out determined to put an end to the
Prophet's life but, on listening to the first part of the 20th chapter, at
his sister's house, his enmity gave place to devotion, and hatred was

changed into admiration. The driving force of the Qur'ān was absolutely irresistible. It flowed as a torrent from the mountain-top and carried away everything with it.

In fact, the transformation wrought by the Holy Qur'ān is unparalleled in the history of the world, and thus its claim to being unique stands as unchallenged to-day as it did thirteen centuries ago. No other reformer has brought about such an entire change in the lives of a whole nation. The Qur'ān found the Arabs worshippers of idols, stones, trees, heaps of sand, and yet, within less than a quarter of a century, the worship of the One God ruled the whole country, idolatry being wiped out from one end to the other. It swept away all superstitions and gave in their place the most rational religion that the world could imagine. The Arab who prided himself in his ignorance had, as if by a magician's wand, become the lover of knowledge, drinking deep at every fountain of learning to which he could get access. This was the direct effect of the teaching of the Qur'ān, which not only appealed to reason, ever and anon, but declared man's thirst for knowledge to be unsatiable, when it directed the Prophet himself to pray:

O my Lord! increase me in knowledge (20:114).

Not only had the Qur'ān swept away the deep vices and barefaced immorality of the Arab; it had also inspired him with a burning desire for the best and noblest deeds in the service of humanity. The burying alive of the daughter, the marriage with a step-mother, and the loose sex relations had given place to equal respect for the offspring, whether male or female, to equal rights of inheritance for father and mother, son and daughter, brother and sister, husband and wife, to the chastest relations of sex and to placing the highest value on sexual morality and the chastity of woman. Drunkenness, to which Arabia had been addicted from time immemorial, disappeared so entirely that the very goblets and vessels which were used for drinking and keeping wine could no more be found and, greatest of all, from an Arabia, the various elements of which were so constantly at war with one another that the whole country was about to perish, being "on the brink of a pit of fire" (3:103), as the Qur'ān so beautifully and so tersely puts it, from an Arabia full of these jarring and warring elements the Qur'ān welded out a nation, a united nation full of life and vigour, before whose onward movement the greatest kingdoms of the world crumbled as if they were but toys before the reality of the new faith.

No faith ever imparted such a new life to its votaries on such a wide scale — a life affecting all branches of human activity; a transformation of the individual, of the family, of the society, of the nation, of the country; an awakening material as well as moral, intellectual as well as spiritual. The Qur'ān effected a transformation of humanity from the lowest depths of degradation to the highest pinnacle of civilization within an incredibly short time where centuries of reformation work had proved fruitless. To its unparalleled nature, testimony is borne by the non-Muslims, sometimes anti-Muslim, historian. Here are a few instances:

> From time beyond memory, Mecca and the whole Peninsula had been steeped in spiritual torpor. The slight and transient influences of Judaism, Christianity, or philosophical inquiry upon the Arab mind had been but as the ruffling here and there of the surface of a quiet lake; all remained still and motionless below. The people were sunk in superstition, cruelty, and vice ... Their religion was a gross idolatry; and their faith the dark superstitious dread of unseen things ... Thirteen years before the Hejira, Mecca lay lifeless in this debased state. What a change had these thirteen years now produced! ... Jewish truth had long sounded in the ears of the men of Medina; but it was not until they heard the spirit-stirring strains of the Arabian Prophet that they too awoke from their slumber, and sprang suddenly into a new and earnest life.[6]

> A more disunited people it would be hard to find, till suddenly, the miracle took place! A man arose who, by his personality and by his claim to direct Divine guidance,

---

6. Muir's *Life of Mohamet,* ch. *vii.*

actually brought about the impossible - namely, the union of all these warring factions.[7]

And yet we may truly say that no history can boast events that strike the imagination in a more lively manner, or can be more surprising in themselves, than those we meet with in the lives of the first Musalmans; whether we consider the Great Chief, or his ministers, the most illustrious of men; or whether we take an account of the manners of the several countries he conquered; or observe the courage, virtue, and sentiments that equally prevailed among his generals and soldiers.[8]

That the best of Arab writers has never succeeded in producing anything equal in merit to the Quran itself is not surprising.[9]

It is the one miracle claimed by Muhammad - his standing miracle, he called it - and a miracle indeed it is.[10]

Never has a people been led more rapidly to civilization, such as it was, than were the Arabs through Islam.[11]

The Qur'ān is unapproachable as regards convincing power, eloquence, and even composition.[12]

And to it was also indirectly due the marvellous development of all branches of science in the Moslem world.[13]

Here, therefore, its merits as a literary production should, perhaps, not be measured by some preconceived maxims of subjective and aesthetic taste, but by the effects which it

---

7. *The Ins and Outs of Mesopotamia*, p. 99.
8. *The Life of Mohamet* by the Count of Boulainvelliers (English Translation), p. 5.
9. Palmer's *Introduction to English Translation of the Quran*, p. lv.
10. Bosworth Smith's *Life of Muhammad*.
11. *New Researches*, by H. Hirschfield, p. 5.
12. *Ibid.*, p. 8.
13. *Ibid.*, p. 9.

produced in Muhammad's contemporaries and fellow-countrymen. If it spoke so powerfully and convincingly to the hearts of his hearers as to weld hitherto centrifugal and antagonistic elements into one compact and well-organized body, animated by ideas far beyond those which had until now ruled the Arabian mind, then its eloquence was perfect, simply because it created a civilized nation out of savage tribes, and shot a fresh woof into the old warp of history.[14]

The marvellous effect produced by the Holy Qur'ān on the minds of those who first came into contact with it, the unparalleled revolution brought about in the world, the upliftment of not one but many nations from the depth of degradation to the height of civilization is, however, not the only characteristic which establishes its claim to uniqueness. It possesses two other characteristics equally unique - the wealth of ideas and the beauty of style - and these two, combined with the effect it produced, are the three things which raise the Qur'ān to an eminence to which no other book has ever aspired and which make an imitation of it impossible. In fact, the effect produced by the Holy Qur'ān is not a magical mystery. It was merely the greatness and reasonableness of the ideas clothed in the best of forms that appealed to the heart of man and, taking deep root in it, became the driving power to the great goal of life. A blaze of light was cast on all the great questions which had hitherto puzzled man, and the way was thus cleared for onward march and progress. Hence it is, that one of the names by which the Holy Book speaks of itself is *al-Burhān*, or the Clear Argument, showing that argument was the weapon which it used to conquer the heart of man; and, as it appealed to reason and not to sentiment, its conquests were far-reaching and permanent. It also speaks of itself as *al-Nūr*, or the Light, and the recipient of this light is called the light-giving sun (33:46) to show that it swept away all mysteries and dispelled all darkness. It is also called *al-Bayān*, or the Explanation, indicating that it had removed all obscurities in religious problems. It claimed not only to have perfected religion (5:3) and thus to have stated all

---

14. Dr. Steingass, in Hugh's *Dictionary of Islam*, art. "Quran."

religious truths needed for the moral and spiritual advancement of man, but also to have dealt with all objections to its truth:

> And they shall not bring to thee any argument but We have brought to thee one with truth and best in explanation (25:33).

A few more words on the outer garb in which the grand life-giving ideas of the Qur'ān are clothed and I shall have done with this subject. The style and diction of the Qur'ān have been universally praised. In the Introduction to his Translation of the Qur'ān, Sale says:

> The Koran is universally allowed to be written with the utmost elegance and purity of language in the dialect of the tribe of Koreish, the most noble and polite of all the Arabians, but with some mixture, though very rare, of other dialects. It is confessedly the standard of the Arabic tongue.

And again:

> The style of the Koran is generally beautiful and fluent ... and in many places, especially where the majesty and attributes of God are described, sublime and magnificent.

What, however, establishes the Qur'ān's claim to uniqueness even in outward form, apart from its subject and the effect produced, is the permanent hold that it has kept on the Arabic language itself, the fact that it remains for ever the standard by which the beauty of style and diction may be judged in Arabic literature. No other book in the world can be credited with even the achievement of keeping alive a language for thirteen centuries; the Qur'ān has done this, attaining to the eminence of being the standard of eloquence for so long, and of retaining that position while the nation speaking it emerged from oblivion to become the leader of civilization in the world, leaving its home to settle in far distant lands where Arabic became either the spoken language of the masses or at least their literary language. Such is the incredible achievement of the Holy Qur'ān. It is true that the Arabs had a literary language before the Qur'ān — the language of poetry, which, notwithstanding slight dialectic differences, conformed to one standard - but the scope of that poetry was very limited. Their most eloquent themes rarely went beyond the praise of wine or woman and horse or sword. In the condition in which Arabic was before the advent of Islam, it would soon have shared the fate of the sister languages of the Semitic group. It was the Qur'ān which made it the language of a civilized world from the Oxus to the Atlantic. Whatever changes spoken Arabic like any other language may have undergone, literary Arabic is to this day the Arabic of the Qur'ān, and the Qur'ān remains its one masterpiece.

European criticism has generally blundered in its opinion that the eloquence of the Qur'ān is not maintained to the last and that the force of the first revelations is not seen in later revelations. The earlier Makka revelation is said to be rhetorical, while the later Makka revelation and the Madina revelation are said to be prosaic and less enthusiastic. This division is fantastic, not real. If, in calling the earlier revelation rhetorical, there is any insinuation that the language is made artificially forceful to produce an effect on the minds of hearers, the statement is utterly erroneous. The one characteristic of the Qur'ān is its freedom from artificiality. The language is simple and natural. It is also forceful, but it is the forcefulness of the natural flow, like the flow of the torrent from a height. "Sincerity," as Carlyle puts it, "sincerity, in all senses, seems to me the merit of the Qur'ān." It is rhetorical in the sense that the grand ideas clothed in beautiful language as conveyed by the Holy Qur'ān did influence the minds of men and do influence them now; but in this respect no distinction can be made between earlier and later revelations. As I have already quoted from Dr. Steingass, if the effect produced on the minds of the hearers did not diminish as years went on — it, in fact, increased — then there is not the least reason for the assertion that the eloquence of the Qur'ān was not maintained, its powerfulness and its convincing force being a clear indication of its eloquence. Certainly the eloquence of the later revelation is of a different nature from that of the first revelation, and the difference is due to the difference of the subject-matter. The early Makka revelations of the Qur'ān deal with that grand theme, the power, majesty, and glory of God and His judgment of good and evil, and the subject-matter lends a loftiness and grandeur to the composition. A description of the power and glory of God must be grand, whether in the Vedas or the Bible or the Qur'ān, but in the Qur'ān its grandeur is simply unapproachable, because the ideas are loftier than those in any other book. The shortness of the sentences is, however, due to their affirmatory or prophetical nature; it is like the seed giving forth its first blossom which is naturally small and delicate in comparison with the form which it achieves later. Here there is an appeal to human nature, an appeal to man to think and reflect, to see within himself. Here the Divine judgment of good and evil is very often described in the form of a prophecy. These characteristics of the subject and the method in which it is dealt with make the style of the earlier revelation what it is — sublime, enthusiastic, fascinating, pithy.

Truth, however, had to be established by every possible means. The hand of God is working everywhere; Divine judgment is near at hand, in fact working every moment; such was the assertion, and it had to be strengthened. There are short references to earlier history in the earliest revelations, but this phase had now to be elaborated. How Divine judgment of good and evil had been working in the history of the world, had to be explained. Hence, later revelation deals at great length with the histories of the previous people, and the nature of the style adopted is necessarily changed. The appeal is still as effective as in the earlier revelation — it is only in another direction.

There is yet a third phase upon which revelation enters after the flight to Madina. The object of revelation was to bring about a change in the life of the individual and in the life of the nation. The object of the earlier Makka revelation was to produce a living belief in the majesty and power of God and in the reality of the Divine judgment of good and evil, such a belief inspiring man with the motive-power which could enable him to attain the object of his life. The Madina revelation, on the other hand, was needed to point out the way itself. The goal of life could not be attained unless the various faculties with which man was endowed were developed fully in the right direction, and hence a guidance was needed in every sphere of life. The details of law were, therefore, as necessary to make man reach the goal of life as a conviction of the power and majesty of God, but the revelation giving these details could not follow the style and diction of the earlier revelation, nor could its excellence be judged by the same standard. Dr. Steingass has dealt with this point so beautifully that I cannot resist the temptation of giving a somewhat lengthy quotation from him:

> But if we consider the variety and heterogeneousness of the topics on which the Qur'ān touches, uniformity of style and diction can scarcely be expected; on the contrary, it would appear to be strangely out of place. Let us not forget that in the book, as Muhammad's newest biographer Ludolf Krehl expresses it, 'there is given a complete code of creeds and morals, as well as of the law based thereupon. There are also the foundations laid for every institution of an extensive commonwealth, for instruction, for the administration of justice, for military organization, for the finances, for a most careful legislation for the poor: all built up on the belief in the One God, Who holds man's destinies in His hand.' Where so many important objects are concerned, the standard of excellence by which we have to gauge the composition of the Quran as a whole must needs vary with the matter treated upon in each particular case. Sublime and chaste, where the supreme truth of God's unity is to be proclaimed; appealing in high-pitched strains to the imagination of a poetically gifted people, where the eternal consequences of man's submission to God's holy will, or of rebellion against it, are pictured; touching in its simple, almost crude, earnestness, when it seeks again and again encouragement or consolation for God's messenger and a solemn warning for those to whom he has been sent, in the histories of the prophets of old: the language of the Quran adapts itself to the exigencies of everyday life, where this everyday life, in its private and public bearings, is to be brought into harmony with the fundamental principles of the new dispensation.

Here, therefore, its merits as a literary production should, perhaps, not be measured by some preconceived maxims of subjective and aesthetic taste, but by the effects which it produced on Muhammad's contemporaries and fellow-countrymen. If it spoke so powerfully and convincingly to the hearts of his hearers as to weld hitherto centrifugal and antagonistic elements into one compact and well-organized body, animated by ideas far beyond those which had until now ruled the Arabian mind, then its eloquence was perfect, simply because it created a civilized nation out of savage tribes, and shot a fresh woof into the old warp of history.[15]

---

15. Hughe's *Dictionary of Islam*, art. "Quran."

Chapter 2
Essentials of Religion
Section 1
Unity of God

The Unity of the Divine Being is the point on which the greatest stress is laid in the Holy Qur'ān. It is with a declaration of the Unity of God that the Holy Book opens and it is with a declaration of His Unity that it ends. It is the one topic which runs through every page and every line of it. In connection with the Quranic teaching on this point, I will draw attention to three points.

The first point is that the doctrine of Divine Unity was restored to its original purity by the Qur'ān. The Holy Book lays it down that every prophet taught the Unity of God and that this doctrine was the original basis of all religions. The first message of every prophet to his people, according to the Qur'ān, was:

> Serve God, you have no god other than Him (7:59, 65, 73, 85);

or,

> You shall not serve any but God (11:26, 50, 61, 84),

and so on; and this doctrine is described as the universal teaching of all the prophets:

> And We did not send before thee any apostle but We revealed to him that there is no god but Me, therefore serve Me (21:25).

Again and again, speaking of polytheism, it asks the upholders of that doctrine, if they have authority sent down to them by God:

42

Have they taken gods besides Him? Say, Bring your proof (21:24);

Have We given them a book before it so that they hold fast to it (43:21).

At the same time it tells us that the doctrine of Unity was mixed up with polytheism by all religions, and to this general corruption it refers in 30:41: "Corruption has appeared in land and sea."

Having established that the Unity of God was taught by every prophet who appeared in any part of the world and that polytheistic doctrines were introduced afterwards into the teachings of the prophets, the Holy Qur'ān invites the followers of all religions to come back to that pure teaching as the basis of an understanding:

Say, O followers of the Book! come to an equitable proposition between us and you that we shall not serve any but God and that we shall not associate aught with Him and that some of us shall not take others for lords besides God (3:64).

Now it must be borne in mind that according to the Holy Qur'ān, prophets appeared among all the nations of the world, and, therefore, all the nations are the people of the Book. The verse quoted above, therefore, requires all the nations of the world to come to an understanding by finding out the common element in the different religions, and that common element would form the basis of a religion of humanity. In other words, it lays down that the part which is peculiar to each religion, be it the divinity of Christ or Rama or Krishna or Ahraman, is a later overgrowth, while the part which is common to all, *i.e.* the existence and oneness of God, is the pure teaching of the prophets. This common element, the Unity of God, was thus in its pristine purity re-established by the Holy Qur'ān.

The second point is that the doctrine of Divine Unity was made perfect by the Holy Qur'ān. Judaism no doubt taught that "thou shalt have no gods before Me" or that "thou shalt not make unto thee any graven image" but the Hindu scriptures do not contain even such an express injunction, while Christianity had little to add to the Jewish doctrine. It was the Holy Qur'ān that cast full light on the doctrine of

Divine Unity. It is in one of the earliest chapters that the doctrine of Divine Unity finds the clearest expression in four short sentences:

> Say, He, God, is One; God is He on Whom all depend: He begets not, nor is He begotten: and none is like Him (ch. 112).

These four short sentences negative the four kinds of polytheism that prevailed in the world before Islam - a belief in the plurality of gods or the plurality of persons in Godhead, a belief that other things possess the perfect attributes of the Divine Being, a belief that anyone may be specially related to Him as son or father, and a belief that others may do what is ascribable only to the Divine Being. Again, the Holy Qur'ān condemns the worship of great and learned men, a disease to which otherwise monotheistic nations were prone: "They have taken their doctors of law and their monks for lords besides God" (9:31), where both the Jews and the Christians are spoken of. Thus saint-worship and the worship of learned men was also declared to be opposed to pure monotheism. Undue reverence for great men is also condemned here, for the Prophet, on a question, explained that the Jews and the Christians were spoken of as taking their learned men as lords because they blindly followed what they said. Again, most men who do not appear to bow before images or worship other false gods or fellow-men bow down before the image of self, that greatest of demi-gods. Hence to bring the doctrine of Divine Unity to perfection, the Holy Qur'ān condemned this phase of polytheism in equally strong terms: "Hast thou seen him who takes his low desires for his god?" (25:43).

The third important point in connection with the doctrine of Divine Unity as taught in the Holy Qur'ān is that it does not there remain a mere religious dogma. Instead, it is taught as a principle of action to be carried into practice, and is made the basis of the advancement of humanity to a higher goal. In fact, *īmān* (belief) according to the Holy Qur'ān is not simply a conviction of the truth of a given proposition; it is essentially the acceptance to a proposition as a basis for action. "Those who believe and do good" is the ever-recurring description of the believers and, in making belief and actions so closely related to each other, the Qur'ān has shown that no belief is acceptable unless it is carried into practice. It is for this reason that even the believers are asked to believe:

> O you who believe! believe in God and His Apostle (4:136);
>
> O you who believe! be careful of your duty to God and believe in His Apostle (57:28).

A belief in any doctrine is meaningless unless that belief is made the basis of an action and this is what is meant by calling upon the believers to believe.

Such is also the belief in the Unity of God. The idea that man shall not bow before others than God because the Lord God is a jealous God finds no place in the Qur'ān. Nay, _shirk_ (associating gods with God) is condemned because it demoralizes man, and Divine Unity is taught because it brings about the moral elevation of man. Belief in Divine Unity does not in any way add to the glory of God, nor does _shirk_ detract from it in the least. Man is described in the Holy Qur'ān as _khalīfa_ or vicegerent of God, to show that he is gifted with the power of controlling the rest of creation (2:30). He is thus placed above the whole of creation, even above the angels, who make obeisance to him (2:34). He is told expressly that he has been made to rule the world:

> God is He Who made subservient to you the sea that the ships may run therein by His command and that you may seek of His grace, and that you may give thanks. And He has made subservient to you whatsoever is in the heavens and whatsoever is in the earth, all from Himself; surely there are signs in this for a people who reflect (45:12, 13).

If, then, man has been created to rule the universe, and he is gifted with the power and capabilities to subdue everything and to turn it to his use, does he not degrade himself by taking other things for gods, by bowing before the elements of nature which he has been created to conquer and rule? This is the view of Divine Unity which the Holy Qur'ān expressly puts forth. It denounces _shirk_ because _shirk_ degrades man and makes him unfit for the high place for which he has been created. It is full of statements like the following:

> If thou shouldst associate anything (with God), thy work would certainly come to naught and thou wouldst certainly be of the losers (39:65);

> And whoever associates anything with God he indeed strays off into a remote error (4:116).

Man's high place in creation is clearly advanced in many places as an argument against _shirk_. Thus the words in 6:164: "Say, What! shall I seek a lord other than God and He is the Lord of all things?" are followed in the next verse by the argument: "And He has made you rulers of the earth." Again it says:

> What! shall I seek for you a god other than God while He has made you excel all created things? (7:140).

The argument is too clear to need explanation. Man is endowed with faculties and powers which can make him excel all creation; if he stoops before the very things which are made subservient to him, he makes himself unfit for attaining the high position which is meant for him in the Divine scheme.

Thus, in its message of Divine Unity, Islam opens out before man a vast field of advancement. It tells him that he is gifted with vast capabilities and that he occupies the highest position in this world. If, however, he occupies such a high position, if he is the vicegerent of God on earth, if he can rise to the highest place in creation, may not the man who has actually attained to that high dignity, the super-man, be taken for an object of worship? The Holy Qur'ān tells us that even that would lower the dignity of man. The super-man to whom was revealed this message of the dignity of man was told to add to the ennobling message of the doctrine of Divine Unity, so beautifully and yet so succinctly summed up in the four words _lā ilāha ill-Allāh_, another equally ennobling message, that the greatest of men, Muhammad (may peace and the blessings of God be upon him) was only a servant of God like all other men, a mortal in no way differing from them except that he was the bearer of that wonderful message to humanity — _Muhammad-un Rasūl Ullāh_:

> Say, I am only a mortal like you; it is revealed to me that your God is one God; so whoever hopes to meet his Lord, he

should do good deeds, and not join anyone in the service of his Lord (18:110).

Thus, from the doctrine of Divine Unity, springs the equally important doctrine that all men are alike, or the doctrine of the unity of the human race. Man was freed not only from the slavery of nature to which he had hitherto been subject but from a still greater slavery, the slavery of man. The bonds were cut which enslaved the mind of man, and he was set on the road to progress. A slave mind, as the Holy Qur'ān says plainly, is incapable of doing anything good and great (16:75, 76); hence the first condition for the advancement of man was that his mind should be set free from the trammels of slavery, and this was accomplished by the Holy Qur'ān in its message of Divine Unity.

The doctrine of Divine Unity as preached by the Qur'ān may now briefly be stated as follows: that there is the Supreme Being, Creator, and Lord of all, Who alone is to be worshipped and from Whom alone help is to be sought; that man is endowed with vast capabilities so that he can conquer and subjugate the forces of nature and make them serve his purpose, and that all men are equal. To carry these principles into practice, the Muslims are enjoined, on the one hand, to pray to God and, on the other, to reflect on His creation:

> In the creation of the heavens and the earth and the alternation of the night and the day there are surely signs for men of understanding: those who remember God, standing and sitting and lying on their sides and reflect on the creation of the heavens and the earth (3:190, 191).

The wise ones are here described as possessing two characteristics: they remember God and they reflect on the creation of the heavens and the earth. Reflection on things clearly stands for scientific pursuits, for science is nothing but knowledge gained by systematic observation, experiment, and reasoning, and it is to this that the Holy Qur'ān calls attention when it points out that the right course of those endowed with understanding is that they should observe all that has been created, whether it is on the earth or in the heavens, and ponder over it. To men of understanding it thus recommends the remembrance of God with the pursuit of sciences, combining moral greatness with material advancement, spirituality with science.

Hence it was that Islam gave an impetus to learning and science which is not met with in the history of any other religion. In the history of Christianity, for instance, we find that it started with monasticism and asceticism as the way to perfection. Yet what a strange contrast it is that it has ended in the grossest materialism. There was a time in the history of Christianity when the pursuit of science was considered to be the greatest of crimes, but now Christendom is so engrossed in the world and its pursuits that no room has been left for God. The Qur'ān adheres to the middle course and, in consonance with its interpretation of the doctrine of Divine Unity, requires the conquest of nature along with submission to God. Remembrance of God or prayer to Him is, according to the Qur'ān, the means to moral perfection, while reflection on His creation leads to material advancement, and the two are closely related. Man could not conquer nature unless he ceased to bow before it, unless his mind was freed from servility to things lower than himself; but with his conquest of nature came his material advancement and, to keep the balance even, it was necessary that he should at the same time attain to moral greatness, which could be brought about only by remembrances of God, by the holding of communion with the Supreme, All-pervading Spirit. The remembrance of God, it should be borne in mind, does not mean the utterance of the name of God on a rosary; it stands for the realization of the Divine within the man, or for the acquirement of the Divine attributes. The *salāt*, or prayer of Islam, which is another name for *dhikr*, or the remembrance of God, is a means to the same end. It is the way by which communion is sought with God, and the object in view is to drink deep from the fountain of Divine attributes and to imbibe the Divine morals. The pursuit of science and worldly occupations are thus combined with the attainment of spiritual and moral greatness in Islam, both being really different aspects of a belief in Divine Unity, when the principle is brought into practice.

Another practical aspect of the doctrine of Divine Unity, as dealt with in the Holy Qur'ān, is the unity of the human race. "One God" has its parallel in "One Humanity." The idea of the unity of the human race, on which alone depends its advancement to a higher goal of life, was as entirely lost to the world before the Qur'ān as the idea of the Unity of God. How could there be any unity of the human race when each nation considered itself to be the only favoured nation, the only recipient of Divine revelation, to the exclusion of all other nations who were for ever condemned to the wrath of God? The Holy Qur'ān came with an entirely new message. It revealed a God who was not the God of this or that nation but who was *Rabb al-'ālamīn*, the Lord, the Sustainer and the Nourisher, of all the nations and of all the worlds. The Qur'ān never speaks of the Lord of the Arabs or of the Lord of the Muslims. The God of the Qur'ān is the Lord of the worlds (1:1), the Lord of the heavens and of the earth (37:5), the Lord of the easts and of the wests (70:40). He is the Lord of the Muslims as well as of the non-Muslims, the Lord even of the enemies of the Muslims:

> I am commanded to do justice between you: God is our Lord and your Lord; we shall have our deeds and you shall have your deeds (42:15).

And again:

> Do you dispute with us about God and He is our Lord and your Lord (2:139).

And still again:

> Say, We believe in that which has been revealed to us and that which has been revealed to you, and our God and your God is One (29:46).

No more ennobling message could be given to humanity. Men and nations may differ, even fight, with one another but they had only one Father, one Lord, one God. No nation was the favourite nation, because all were equal recipients of that greatest of Divine favours, the blessing of Divine revelation. As God was One so was humanity one.

> All people are a single nation (2:213).

> And people are naught but a single nation (10:19),

was the grand message of the new revelation. The whole of humanity was only one nation. The division into tribes and families did not in any way interfere with this vast brotherhood of humanity:

> O you men! We have created you of a male and a female, and made you tribes and families that you may know one another; surely the most honourable of you with God is the one among you most careful of his duty (49:13).

This is the true brotherhood of the human race, and the day when this broad conception of a human nationality and human brotherhood is accepted, petty national jealousies will come to an end, and a new era of peace and progress will dawn upon the world.

Section 2
Divine Attributes

The word *Allāh* is used in the Holy Qur'ān as the proper name of the Divine Being, while He is mentioned by a number of other names, every one of which refers to one of His attributes, *Allāh* comprising all the attributes by which He is known. *Allāh* is an underived word, and is not a contraction of *al-ilāh* (the god). It has never been applied to any being except the only true God, nor did the Arabs ever give this name to any of their idols. As a proper name it cannot be translated into any other language nor is an equivalent of it met with in any other language; hence, whatever language the Muslims speak in any part of the world, they all speak of the Supreme Being as *Allāh*. The word God in the English language is not a substitute for *Allāh*, but it has been used for the facility of the English reader. The word *Allāh*, occurring 2,799 times, is, of all the names of the Divine Being, the most frequently recurring in the Holy Qur'ān.

Before speaking of the attributes of God mentioned in the Holy Qur'ān, it is necessary to warn the reader against a misconception about the nature of the Divine Being. God is spoken of in the Holy Qur'ān as seeing, hearing, speaking, making, showing mercy, being displeased, loving, being affectionate, etc., but the use of these words is by no means an indication of an anthropomorphic conception of God; for, He is plainly stated to be above all material conceptions:

> Vision comprehends Him not and He comprehends all vision (6:103).

He is not only above all material limitations but even above the limitation of metaphor:

> Nothing is like a likeness of Him (42:11).

Such is the transcendentally pure conception of the Divine Being. Hence the rule is laid down clearly that, though the words in which

51

the acts of God are spoken of, are the same as those in which the acts of man are referred to, yet there is this essential difference in the two cases that the agent or instrument which enables a man to perform a deed is not conceived of in the case of God.

Of the attributes of the Divine Being, the one that occupies the first place in the Holy Qur'ān is *Rabb* which, for want of a proper word, is translated as *Lord*. The word in Arabic, however, carries a far grander idea than its English rendering. Its significance, according to Raghib, is the *fostering a thing in such a manner as to make it attain one condition after another until it reaches its goal of completion*. Hence *Rabb* is the Lord Who not only gives to the whole creation its means of sustenance, but has also preordained for each kind a sphere of capacity and, within that sphere, provided the means by which it continues gradually to attain its goal of perfection. This significance, given by an Arab lexicographer long before the theory of evolution was known, shows that the idea of evolution is present in the first attribute of the Divine Being mentioned in the Holy Qur'ān. The importance of this attribute among all the others is clear from the fact that it is the first attribute mentioned in the Holy Qur'ān in its present arrangement, occurring in the first verse of the opening chapter after the name *Allāh*; it is the attribute mentioned in the first revelation granted to the Holy Prophet, occurring twice in the first five verses of the 96th chapter; it is the attribute which, after *Allāh*, is mentioned most frequently, occurring 965 times in the Holy Qur'ān; and, lastly, it is the name by which God is most often addressed in prayers.

It may be noted here that the Qur'ān adopts the word *Rabb* instead of the word *ab* (meaning *father*) which was frequently used by Jesus Christ in addressing God, because the significance carried by the word *ab* is very limited in comparison with the grand idea contained in the word *Rabb*. Another peculiarity regarding this attribute may be noted here. It is never used absolutely but always as my *Rabb* or our *Rabb* or your *Rabb*, or thy *Rabb* or *Rabb* of the world. The reason is plain. The Nourisher or Sustainer can be spoken of only in relation to something which He nourishes or sustains. He is spoken of repeatedly as the *Rabb* (or Sustainer) of believers as well as of unbelievers, of the Muslims as well as of their opponents, which is a clear evidence of the broadness of the conception of God in Islam.

Next to *Rabb* in importance are the closely-related names *Raḥmān* and *Raḥīm*, translated as Beneficent and Merciful respectively. They occur 400 times in the Qur'ān, while the same attribute in verb form — *showing of mercy* — occurs about 170 times, bringing the total to about 570. No other attribute, with the exception of *Rabb*, is as frequently repeated. These two attributes not only occupy the highest place after *Rabb* with regard to the frequence of their occurrence, but their importance is also indicated by bringing them in immediately after the attribute *Rabb* in the opening chapter, and further by heading with them every chapter of the Holy Qur'ān in the well-known formula *Bismillāh-ir-Raḥmān-ir-Raḥīm*. Both these words are active participle nouns of different forms from the same root *raḥma*, which signifies *tenderness requiring the exercise of beneficence*, and thus comprises the idea of *love* and *mercy*. *Raḥmān* is of the type of *fa'lān* and indicates the greatest preponderance of the quality of mercy, and *Raḥīm* is of the type of *fa'īl* and expresses a constant repetition and manifestation of that quality. The two words are applicable to two different states of the exercise of mercy in God; the first to that state when man has not done anything to deserve it and God exercises His unbounded mercy in bestowing His gifts on him, and the second to that condition when man does something to deserve His mercy, and His mercy is, therefore, repeatedly exercised for him. Thus it is *Raḥmān* Who creates for man all those things which make his life possible on this earth, and it is *Raḥīm* Who gives him the fruits of his labour; or, again, it is *Raḥmān* Who, by His revelation, shows man the right way to develop his faculties, and it is *Raḥīm* Who rewards the faithful for the good they do.

This distinction is so fine that Church Christianity has been unable to realize it, for it holds that God could not show mercy unless man had done something to deserve it, and hence the necessity for a vicarious atonement. Verses 19:88-92 may be specially noted in this connection where the allegation "the Beneficent God has taken Himself a son" is met with the argument: "And it is not worthy of the Beneficent God that He should take to Himself a son", the implication being that the mercy of the Beneficent God (*Raḥmān*) was so unbounded that He could show mercy even to those who had done nothing to deserve it.

It is not only the frequent occurrence of the two names *Raḥmān* and *Raḥīm* and the importance attached to them by placing them at the head of each chapter that shows that the quality of mercy is, according to the Holy Qur'ān, the most predominant of all qualities in God, but the Holy Book has gone further and laid the greatest stress in explicit words on the immeasurable vastness of Divine mercy. I quote only a few examples:

> He has ordained mercy on Himself (6:12).

> Your Lord has ordained mercy on Himself (6:54).

> Your Lord is the Lord of all-encompassing mercy (6:147).

> And My mercy encompasses all things (7:156).

> In the grace of God and in His mercy they should rejoice (10:58).

> Except those on whom thy Lord has mercy, and for this did He create them (11:119).

> O My servants! who have acted extravagantly against their own souls, do not despair of the mercy of God, for God forgives the sins altogether (39:53).

> Our Lord! Thou embracest all things in mercy and knowledge (40:7).

So great is Divine mercy that it encompasses the believer and the unbeliever alike. Even the opponents of the Prophet are spoken of as having mercy shown to them:

> And when We make people taste of mercy after an affliction touches them, lo! they devise plans against Our communications (10:21).

Whenever the polytheists are spoken of as calling upon God in distress, we are told that God removes their distress and has mercy on them. Again, we find it repeatedly stated that the evil done by man is either obliterated or punished only with the like of it, but good is rewarded tenfold, hundredfold, even without measure. All this proves that, according to the Holy Qur'ān, mercy is the preponderating attribute of God. In fact, the name *Rabb* (the Giver of sustenance) is also indicative of Divine mercy, for providing for His creatures, whether they deserve it or not, is due to His unbounded mercy alone.

The next name in point of importance is *Ghafūr* (Forgiving) so far as the frequence of its occurrence in the Holy Qur'ān is concerned, for, along with the other cognate forms *Ghāfir* and *Ghaffār*, and along with its verb forms indicating the exercise of the attribute of *ghafr*, it occurs 233 times in the Holy Qur'ān. Now *Forgiving* is again a defective rendering for the original *Ghafūr*, for the Arabic word carries a double significance. The root word *ghafr* means the *granting of protection*, and *Ghafūr*, therefore, means the *Grantor of protection against sin* or *against the punishment of sin*. *Forgiving* carries only the latter meaning, and the other significance, which is really the more important, *viz.*, that God is also He Who grants protection to His servants against the commission of sin, is not covered by it. Another point which must be borne in mind in this connection is that God's attribute of forgiveness towards man is not limited by any consideration; the sins may be few or many and the sinful one may be a Muslim or a non-Muslim; see 39:53 quoted above. Nay, He is spoken of as "the Forgiver of sins and the Accepter of repentance" (40:3), so that He forgives even if there is no repentance. Elsewhere He is described as "Worthy to forgive" (74:56), which is explained as meaning that, even if man is not worthy of being forgiven, yet the quality of forgiveness is exercised towards him because God is worthy to forgive. Such is the vastness of the conception of forgiveness of God as taught by the Holy Qur'ān.

I now wish to draw the reader's attention to one notable point. It will be noticed that the attributes of God which most frequently occur in the Holy Qur'ān are also those which are given in the opening chapter which is looked upon as the quintessence of the

Holy Qur'ān, and further that they occur there exactly in the order of their importance. *Allāh*, the proper name occurs 2,799 times and comes first; *Rabb*, occurring 967 times, comes next; *Rahmān* and *Rahīm*, occurring over 560 times, follow *Rabb*. However, the fourth attribute mentioned in the opening chapter is not *Ghafūr* or *Forgiving*, which, after the above three names, occurs most frequently in the Holy Qur'ān; instead of that we have *Mālik* or *Master* (of the day of requital). The reason is that the name *Mālik* or Master is used here, and not king or judge, which names do occur elsewhere in the Holy Qur'ān, to lay stress on the attribute of forgiveness. A judge, or a king in his capacity as a judge, is bound to do justice, and he cannot forgive the offender, but a master has as much right to forgive as to punish. It is the duty of a judge to hold the balance equally between two parties, and God is a judge no doubt; but He is more than a judge; He is the Master, and the guilty are only His creatures whom He can forgive, to whatever extent He pleases, without any suggestion of injustice or favouritism being attributed to Him. The first three attributes of the Divine Being as mentioned in the opening chapter are all attributes expressing the unbounded love and mercy of God for His creatures, but the picture drawn there would have been incomplete if it had left out altogether the punishment of the evil-doers. Nevertheless, punishment is referred to in a word in which the preponderating idea is still that of forgiveness and love, for it is a Master's dealing with His servants and creatures, thus showing that, though punishment is necessary, yet in the Divine scheme it is meted out only when the ends of justice would fail altogether without it, and even then it is a remedial measure.

All the other attributes of the Divine Being that are mentioned in the Holy Qur'ān are, as it were, offshoots of any one of the four essential attributes mentioned in the opening chapter. He is *al-Wāhid* or *Ahad* (the One), *al-Hayy* (the Ever-Living), *al-Qayyūm* (the Self-Subsisting), *al-Ghanī* (the Self-Sufficient), *al-Awwal* (the First), *al-Akhir* (the Last), *al-Quddūs* (the Holy), *al-Samad* (on Whom all depend and He depends not on any), *al-Haqq* (the True).

As relating to the act of creation, He is *al-Khāliq* (the Creator), *al-Bāri'* (the Maker or the Creator of soul), *al-Muṣawwir* (the Fashioner of shapes), *al-Badī'* (Wonderful Originator).

In relation to His love and mercy, He is *al-Ra'ūf* (the Affectionate), *al-Wadūd* (Loving-Kind), *al-Laṭīf* (the Benignant), *al-Tawwāb* (the Oft-Returning to mercy), *al-Ḥalīm* (the Forbearing), *al-'Afuww* (the Pardoner), *al-Shakūr* (the Multiplier of rewards), *al-Salām* (the Author of peace), *al-Mu'min* (the Granter of security), *al-Muhaimin* (the Guardian over all), *al-Jabbār* (the Restorer of every loss), *al-Barr* (the Benign), *Rāfi'al-darajāt* (the Exalter of ranks), *al-Wāsi'* (the Ample-Giving), *al-Wahhāb* (the great Giver), *al-Razzāq* (the Bestower of sustenance).

In relation to His glory, power, and greatness, He is *al-'Aẓīm* (the Great), *al-'Azīz* (the Mighty), *al-Qādir* or *Qadīr* or *Muqtadir* (the Powerful), *al-'Aliyy* or *Muta'āl* (the High), *al-Qawiyy* (the Strong), *al-Qahhār* (the Supreme), *al-Mutakabbir* (the Possessor of every greatness), *al-Kabīr* (the Great), *al-Karīm* (the Honoured), *al-Ḥamīd* (the Praiseworthy), *al-Majīd* (the Glorious), *al-Matīn* (the Strong), *al-Ẓāhir* (the Ascendant over all), *dhul-Jalāl wal Ikrām* (the Lord of glory and honour).

In relation to His knowledge, He is *al-'Alīm* (the Knowing), *al-Hakīm* (the Wise), *al-Samī'* (the Hearing), *al-Khabīr* (the Aware), *al-Baṣīr* (the Seeing), *al-Shahīd* (the Witness), *al-Raqīb* (the Watcher), *al-Bāṭin* (the Knower of hidden things).

In relation to His control of things, He is *al-Wakīl* (having all things in His charge), *al-Waliyy* (the Guardian), *al-Hafīẓ* (the Keeper), *al-Malik* (the King), *al-Mālik* (the Master), *al-Fattāḥ* (the greatest Judge), *al-Hasīb* or *Hāsib* (One who takes account), *al-Muntaqim* or *dhu-Intiqām* (the Inflictor of retribution), *al-Muqīt* (the Controller of all things).

Section 3

Life After Death

According to the Holy Qur'ān, death does not bring the life of man to an end; it only opens the door to a higher form of life. Just as from dust is evolved the man, from the deeds which man does is evolved the higher man. Hence we find the Holy Qur'ān again and again referring to his creation from a very low origin, when speaking of life after death:

> We have created you, why do you not then accept the truth? Have you considered the life-germ? Is it you that create it, or are We the Creator? We have ordained death among you and We are not to be overcome, that We may change your attributes and make you grow into what you know not (56:57-61).

Such is the next life. As from the small life-germ grows up the man and he does not lose his individuality for all the changes which he undergoes, so from this man is made the higher man, his attributes being changed and he being made to grow into what he cannot conceive at present. Man's life in this world is not without an aim, and the aim is to attain to a higher life:

> Does man think that he is to be left to wander without an aim? Was he not a small life-germ in the seminal elements? Then he was a clot of blood, so He created (him) and made (him) perfect; then He made of him two kinds, the male and the female. Is He not able to give life to the dead? (75:36-40).

The life after death is, therefore, one of the fundamentals of Islam, but not as a dogma. On the other hand, it opens out a wide vista of progress before man, a new world of advancement before which the progress of this life sinks into insignificance:

And whoever desires the hereafter, and strives for it as he ought to strive and he is a believer, their striving shall be recompensed ... See how We have made some of them to excel others, and certainly the hereafter is much superior in respect of degrees and much superior in respect of excellence (17:19-21).

And when thou seest thither, thou shalt see blessings and a great kingdom (76:20).

The connection between the two lives, the life on this earth and the life after death, is established in the clearest words. Heaven and hell are not places of enjoyment and torture to be met with only after death; they are realities even here. The hereafter is not a mystery beyond the grave; it begins in this very life. For the good, the heavenly life, and for the wicked, a life in hell, begins even here, and as there are two paradises for the former, there are two chastisements for the latter, *i.e.*, a paradise and a chastisement for this life, and a paradise and a chastisement for the next:

And for him who fears to stand before his Lord are two gardens (55:46).

O soul that art at rest! return to thy Lord, well-pleased with Him, well-pleasing Him: so enter among My servants and enter into My paradise (89:27-30).

Nay, if you had known with a certain knowledge, you should certainly have seen the hell (102:5, 6).

It is the fire kindled by God, which rises above the hearts (104:6, 7).

And whoever is blind in this, shall also be blind in the hereafter (17:72).

And certainly We will make them taste of the nearer chastisement before the greater chastisement that haply they may turn (32:21).

Such is the chastisement and certainly the chastisement of the hereafter is greater, did they but know (68:33).

The resurrection or the Hour.

While the life after death is spoken of as a continuation of this life, a particular day is repeatedly mentioned in the Holy Qur'ān, under various names, as the day on which that life finds a complete manifestation. It is called *yaum al-qiyāma*, or the day of the great rising or resurrection (75:1); *yaum al-faṣl*, or the day of decision (77:13); *yaum al-ḥisāb*, or the day of reckoning (38:26); *yaum al-fat-ḥ*, or the day of judgment (32:29); *yaum al-talāq*, or the day of meeting (40:15); *yaum al-jam'*, or the day of gathering together (42:7); *yaum al-khulūd*, or the day of abiding (50:34); *yaum al-khurūj*, or the day of coming forth (50:42); *yaum al-taghābun*, or the day of the manifestation of defects (64:9); *yaum al-dīn*, or the day of requital (1:3); etc; but the most frequently occurring word for the resurrection is *al-sā'a*, which originally means *any portion of time*, and is, therefore, generally rendered as *the hour*. Raghib, the well-known lexicographer of the Qur'ān, says that there are three *sā'as* (hours) in the sense of the resurrection, *viz.*, 1. *kubrā* (or *the greater*), which is the rising up of the people for reckoning; 2. *wusṭā* (or the middle), which is the passing away of one generation; and 3. *ṣughrā* (or the minor), which is the death of the individual. The word is used in all these senses in the Holy Qur'ān. An example of the last, as given by Raghib, occurs in 6:31: "They are indeed in loss who give the lie to the meeting of God until when the hour comes upon them all of a sudden," where the *hour* clearly stands for the death of the person who gives the lie.

As regards the use of the word in the other two senses, it is very frequent, and the two significances are often interchangeable, either sense being applicable. For instance, take 7:182-187, where the doom of the opponents is first clearly spoken of: "And as to those who reject Our communications, We draw them near to destruction by degrees whence they know not" (182), "And that maybe their doom shall have drawn nigh" (185), and then immediately the *hour* is spoken of: "They ask thee about the hour when will be its coming" (187). This sequence makes it clear that the *hour* here is primarily the *doom* of the opponents with which they were being threatened. Again, take the 54th chapter, which opens thus: "The hour drew nigh and the moon did rend asunder." The hour in this case stands for the doom of the Prophet's opponents, for rending asunder of the moon was a miracle of the Holy Prophet which signified the doom of the Quraish, the moon being an emblem of their power. The same word, *al-sā'a*, occurs twice again in the concluding section of the chapter, and in both places stands for the doom of the opponents:

> Do they say, we are a host allied together to help each other? Soon shall the hosts be routed and they shall turn their backs. Nay, the hour is their promised time, and the hour shall be most grievous and bitter (54:44-46).

Bukhari tells us, in his comment on these verses, that when the Holy Prophet was faced with a most serious situation on the day of Badr, the Muslims being in danger of being annihilated by their powerful opponents, and he was praying for their safety, he was reminded of the prophecy contained here and comforted his companions by reciting these verses aloud, showing that by the *hour* here was meant the hour of the enemy's discomfiture, which is called the "the touch of hell" in v. 48.

I have laid stress on this point to show that the Qur'ān speaks clearly of reward and punishment being awarded in this life as well. In other words, it does not ignore this life and relegate everything to the hereafter. The different words which stand for the resurrection are in some sense also applicable to this life; the rising of the dead is sometimes their spiritual resurrection which was to be brought about by the preaching of the Prophet; *the day of decision* also signifies the triumph of truth and the vanquishment of falsehood; *the day of reckoning* is equally the reckoning in this life, and so is *the day of requital; the day of gathering together* is also the day of the gathering together of the opposing forces, and so on. The law of the requital of good and evil affects this life as much as the next, a complete manifestation taking place when the limitations of the body of clay are removed by death; which thus becomes a starting-point for a new and higher life. It is a law that works every moment and will not come into operation on a particular day; even paradise and hell are spoken of as originating with this life. Hence God is repeatedly described as *quick in reckoning* (2:202; 3:19, 199; etc.), meaning that His reckoning is working every moment. Every evil deed leaves its impress on the human mind: "Nay, rather what they do has become like rust upon their hearts" (83:14), so that the consequence follows as soon as a deed is done. Still more plainly:

"And We have made every man's actions to cling to his neck, and We will bring forth to him on the day of resurrection a book which he will find wide open" (17:13).

Thus an action leaves its effect upon man as soon as it is done; only it is not seen by the human eye, but will be palpably manifest in the form of a wide-open book on the day of resurrection, for the veil which covers the eye now, so that it cannot see the finer things, shall then be removed, as the Qur'ān says:

"Certainly thou wert heedless of it, but now We have removed from thee they veil so thy sight to-day is sharp" (50:22).

The law of the requital of good and evil is thus working all the time; only the consequences cannot be seen by the physical eye, but the finer senses granted in the resurrection will see them clearly: "On the day when hidden things shall be made manifest" (86:9).

The law of the requital of good and evil is a comprehensive one:

"He who has done an atom's weight of good shall see it. and he who has done an atom's weight of evil shall see it" (99:7, 8).

So every good deed bears a fruit, and every evil deed bears an evil consequence, whether the doer is a Muslim or a non-Muslim; but, owing to the preponderance of mercy in Divine nature, good brings tenfold fruit, even seven hundredfold or immeasurably great, while evil is either forgiven or recompensed with the like of it. There is a saying of the Holy Prophet to that effect recorded in the Bukhari, and the Holy Qur'ān is full of statements like the following:

"Whoever brings good, he shall have ten (times) like it, and whoever brings evil, he shall be recompensed only with the like of it, and they shall not be dealt with unjustly" (6:160).

The parable of those who spend their property in the way of God is as the parable of a grain growing seven ears with a hundred grains in every ear; and God makes it manifold for whom He pleases; and God is Ample-Giving, Knowing (2:261).

Whoever brings good, he shall have better than it, and whoever brings evil, those who do evil shall not be rewarded for aught except what they did (28:84).

And whatever affliction befalls you, it is on account of what your hands have wrought, and He pardons most (of your faults) (42:30).

The balance.

A man is judged by the preponderance of good or evil in him and it is in this connection that the setting up of a *mizān*, or balance, is spoken of. The words *wazn* and *mizān*, as used in the Holy Qur'ān in this connection, do not indicate weighing with a pair of scales; it is in the wider sense of fulfilling the requirements of justice that they are used. For instance, 57:25 speaks of apostles being sent with the book and the *mizān*, where the *mizān* clearly stands for rules of justice or principles of equity. In fact, that meaning is made clear by the addition of the words "that men may conduct themselves with equity." Again, 55:7 speaks of a *mizān* being set up in nature: "And the heaven, He raised it high, and He made the *mizān*." Here the *mizān* stands for justice, according to well-known commentators. A similar measure or balance is spoken of as being set up to judge man. Is it good that preponderates in him or evil? Here are a few quotations:

> And We will set up a just balance on the day of resurrection, so no soul shall be dealt with unjustly in the least; and though there be the weight of a grain of mustard seed, We will bring it, and sufficient are We to take account (21:47).

> And the measuring out on that day will be just; then as for those whose measure of good deeds is heavy, they shall be successful. And as for those whose measure of good deeds

is light, these it is that have made their souls suffer loss (7:8, 9).

The book of deeds.

A few words may be added as to the *book of deeds*. We are told that every action, however great or small, is written down:

> And the book shall be placed, then thou wilt see the guilty fearing from what is in it; and they will say: Ah! woe to us! what a book is this! it does not omit a small one or a great one, but numbers them all (18:49).

> So whoever shall do of good deeds and he is a believer, there shall be no denying of his exertion, and We write it down for him (21:94).

> He utter not a word but there is by him a watcher at hand (50:18).

> Or do they think that We do not hear what they conceal and their secret discourses? Aye! and Our messengers with them write down (43:80).

> And surely there are keepers over you, honourable recorders - they know what you do (82:10-12).

> This is Our book that speaks against you with justice; surely We wrote what you did (45:29).

Not only has every individual his book of deeds, but even nations are spoken of as having their books of deeds:

> And thou shalt see every nation kneeling down; every nation shall be called to its book — to-day you shall be rewarded for what you did (45:28).

It must, however, be borne in mind that the word *kitāb* (translated as *book*) or *kataba* (he wrote) is used in a very wide sense in the Holy Qur'ān. As Raghib says, *kitāb* (book) does not always mean *a collection of written leaves*; it sometimes signifies *the knowledge of God*, or *His command*, or *what He has made obligatory*. Nor does *kataba* always signify that *he wrote certain words on paper with ink and pen*; it also means *he made a thing obligatory*, or *decreed*, or *ordained*, or *prescribed* a thing. Let us see now what is meant by the writing of the deeds and the book of deeds. The above quotations show that by the writing of the deeds is meant their preserving and guarding, the angels being called both *keepers* and *recorders*. The following verses throw additional light on this subject:

> And We have made every man's actions to cling to his neck, and We will bring forth to him on the resurrection day a book which he will find wide open. Read thy book; they own self is sufficient as a reckoner against thee this day (17:13, 14).

> There are (angels) following him closely, before him and behind him, who guard him by God's command (13:11).

> Nay! the book of the wicked is in the prison. And what will make thee know what the prison is? It is a written book (83:7-9).

> Nay! the book of the righteous is in the highest places. And what will make thee know what the highest places are? It is a written book (83:18-20).

The first of these quotations shows that the book of deeds which a man will find on the resurrection day is nothing but the effect of the deeds he has done. In the second, it is not what a man does that is spoken of as being guarded, but it is clearly the doer who is guarded, and, reading it with the first quotation, the conclusion is evident that man's deeds are guarded by the impress which they make upon him. The third and the fourth quotations show that the book of deeds is identical with the place where it is kept; in the former, the book of deeds is in a prison and the prison is a written book; in the latter, the book of deeds is in the highest places and the highest places are a written book. The book of deeds is, therefore, within the man because the deeds are preserved by the effect which they leave on the man. It is said to be in a prison, in one case, because the evil deeds hamper a man's progress, and keep his faculties for the doing of great and good deeds shut up, as it were, within a prison; and in the other case it is said to be in the highest places, because by good deeds the faculties given to man find their highest development. It is quite in consonance with this that we are told that a man himself will take his own account:

> Read thy book; thy own self is sufficient as a reckoner against thee this day (17:14).

It is sometimes the doer that reads his own book while on another occasion he invites others to read the same:

> Lo! read my book (69:19).

Such is the doer of good, while the evil-doer is made to say:

> O would that my book had never been given me, and I had not known what my account was (69:25, 26).

That each nation has also a book, as already pointed out, bears out the truth of what has been said here, for that impress of what a people do is equally left on their national life, and nations like individuals are judged by what they do.

Section 4
Paradise and Hell

The life after death takes two forms: a life in paradise for those in whom the good preponderates over the evil, and a life in hell for those in whom the evil preponderates over the good. The word *paradise* (Ar. *firdaus*) occurs only twice in the Holy Qur'ān — in 18:107 and 23:11. It is the word *janna* (garden) or its plural *jannāt* that is generally used to indicate the abiding-place of the righteous, who are generally described as those who believe and do good deeds, while their abiding-place is generally said to be gardens in which rivers flow, the rivers corresponding to faith, and the trees of the garden corresponding to the good which a man does. The word *janna* is derived from *jann*, which means *to conceal a thing so that it is not perceived by the senses*, and *janna* means *a garden* because its ground is covered by trees. The description of paradise as a garden with rivers flowing in it is, however, only a parable:

> A parable of the garden which the righteous are promised: therein are rivers of water (47:15).

The blessings of paradise cannot be conceived in this life, and are not, therefore, things of this world:

> No soul knows what is hidden for it of that which will refresh the eyes: a reward for what they did (32:17).

An explanation of these words by the Holy Prophet is given in the *Bukhari* as follows:

> God says, I have prepared for My righteous servants what no eye has seen and no ear has heard, and what the mind of man has not conceived.

Therefore, paradise and what it contains cannot be even conceived by the mind of man. Ibn 'Abbas is reported to have said that "nothing that is in paradise resembles anything that is in this world except in name." For instance, the word _ẓill_ (shade) occurs very often in the Holy Qur'ān in connection with the blessings of paradise, but a shade is not what is really meant, for there is no sun: "They shall see therein neither sun nor intense cold" (76:13). The word is there, but the significance underlying it is different. According to Raghib, it stands for plenty or protection. Such is also _rizq_ (sustenance) in paradise; it cannot be what sustains the body here; in fact, prayer itself is called a sustenance in 20:131. Nor are the fruits of paradise like the fruits of this life, because these are the fruits of the deeds done. 2:25 makes it clear:

> Whenever they shall be given a portion of the fruits thereof, they shall say, This is what was given to us before.

Evidently the fruits of the deeds are meant here, and not the fruits that the earth grows, because the latter are not given to all the faithful here, while the former are. Similar is the case with the water, the milk, the honey, the cushions, the thrones, the clothes and the adornments of the next life; they are not things of this life; these descriptions are of the nature of parables, as the Qur'ān expressly calls them a _mathal_ or a parable.

In fact, a little consideration would show that even our ideas of place and time are not applicable to the next life. It is said in the Qur'ān that paradise extends over the whole of the heavens and the earth:

> And hasten to forgiveness from your Lord and a garden the extensiveness of which is as the heavens and the earth (3:133, 57:21);

and when the Prophet was asked where hell was, if paradise extended over the whole of the heavens and the earth, he replied: "Where is the night when the day comes?" This shows clearly that paradise and hell are more like two conditions than two places. Again, notwithstanding that the two are poles asunder, the one being the highest of the high and the other the lowest of the low, they are separated only by a wall:

> Then a separation would be brought between them by a wall having a door in it; on the inside of it there shall be mercy

and before the outside of it there shall be chastisement (57:13).

Elsewhere, speaking of the inmates of paradise and the inmates of hell, it says: "And between the two there shall be a veil" (7:46). Again, a "vehement raging and roaring" of hell-fire is mentioned repeatedly (25:12; 67:7), but those in paradise shall "not hear its faintest sound" (21:102), while we are told that those in hell shall talk with those in heaven and the two shall hear each other; see 7:44-50. I quote only the concluding verse:

And the inmates of the fire shall call out to the dwellers of the garden, saying: Pour on us some water or of that which God has given you. They shall say: God has prohibited them both to the unbelievers.

Thus those in paradise shall hear the talk of those in hell, but they shall not hear the roaring of the fire of hell. This shows that hell is a condition which shall be perceived only by those in it, and similar is the case with paradise.

Paradise and Hell begin in this life.

As I have already pointed out, the Holy Qur'ān says that paradise and hell begin in this very life. Read the following verses along with those already quoted:

And convey good news to those who believe and do good deeds that they shall have gardens in which rivers flow; whenever they shall be given a portion of the fruits thereof, they shall say, This is what was given to us before; and they shall be given the like of it (2:25).

For them is a known sustenance (37:41).

And He shall cause them to enter the garden which He has made known to them (47:6).

The first of these verses shows that the fruits which the righteous shall find in paradise shall be the same as were given to them in this life; the second and the third show that the sustenance which shall be given to them in paradise is made known to them in this very life. It is clear that the sustenance and the fruits spoken of here are not those

which the righteous have in common with the evil-doers, the fruits
and the sustenance that the earth grows, what is needed for the
support of the body of both. The things meant are those which are
granted specially to the righteous, to which the evil-doers have no
access; in fact, they remain quite blind to them in this life and are,
therefore, deprived of them in the hereafter: "And whoever is blind
in this, shall also be blind in the hereafter" (17:72). These are the
fruits of good deeds and the sustenance which the righteous find in
the remembrance of God. It is the sustenance spoken of in the
following verses and elsewhere:

> Bear them patiently what they say and glorify thy Lord by
> the praising of Him before the rising of the sun and before
> its setting, and during hours of the night do also glorify and
> during parts of the day that thou mayest be well-pleased.
> And do not stretch thy eyes after that with which We have
> provided different classes of them, of the splendour of this
> world's life, that We may thereby try them, and the
> sustenance of they Lord is better and more abiding (20:130,
> 131).

It is in accordance with this that the soul that has found rest in
God is admitted to paradise in this life:

> O soul that art at rest! return to thy Lord, well-pleased with
> Him, well-pleasing Him; so enter among My servants and
> enter into My garden (89:27-30).

It is quite in accordance with this conclusion that we find that the
highest bliss of paradise is plainly stated to be the pleasure of God,
the greatest spiritual blessing which the righteous strive for in this
life, and by attaining which they enter into paradise in this very life,
as has just been shown:

> God has promised to the believing men and the believing
> women gardens in which rivers flow, to abide in them, and
> goodly dwellings in gardens of perpetual abode; and greatest
> of all is God's goodly pleasure - that is the grand
> achievement (9:72).

Those in paradise shall be occupied with and find delight in the praise of God and in His glorification; in what is declared to be a spiritual sustenance for the righteous in this life (20:131):

> Their cry in it shall be, Glory to Thee, O God! and their greeting in it shall be, Peace; and the last of their cry shall be, Praise be to God, the Lord of the worlds (10:10).

There is no grief, fatigue or toil therein, and the heart is purified of all rancour and jealousy, peace and security reigning on all sides:

> The righteous shall be in the midst of gardens and fountains. Enter them in peace, secure. And We will root out whatever of rancour is in their breasts - they shall be as brethren on raised couches, face to face. Toil shall not afflict them in it, nor shall they be ever ejected from it (15:45-48).

> They shall not hear therein vain or sinful discourse, except the word peace, peace (56:25, 26).

> And they shall say: All praise is due to God Who has made grief to depart from us; surely our Lord is forgiving, Multiplier of reward, Who has made us alight in a house abiding for ever out of His grace; toil shall not touch us therein, nor shall fatigue therein afflict us (35:34, 35).

Notwithstanding all this, paradise, according to the Holy Qur'ān, is not a place for simple enjoyment or rest; it is essentially a place for advancement to higher and higher stages:

> But those who are careful of their duty to their Lord, shall have high places, above them higher places, built (for them) (39:20).

This shows that not only does paradise admit the righteous to high places, but it is in fact the starting-point for a new advancement, there being higher and higher places still, and it is in accordance with this that they are spoken of as having an unceasing desire for attaining to higher and higher excellences, their prayer in paradise being: "O our Lord! make perfect for us our light" (66:8). This idea of a ceaseless advancement in paradise is one which is peculiar to the

Holy Qur'ān, and not the least trace of it is to be met with in any other scripture.

Hell meant for purification.

Quite in accordance with the idea of paradise as a place of unending progress to higher stages of life is the idea of hell where punishment is not meant for torture but for purification, in order to make a man fit for spiritual advancement. The idea underlying hell is that those who wasted their opportunity in this life shall, under the inevitable law which makes every man taste of what he has done, be subjected to a course of treatment for the spiritual diseases which they have brought about with their own hands. It is for this reason that the Holy Qur'ān makes a difference between the abiding in paradise and the abiding in hell, allowing a termination in the latter case but not in the former.

As I have already noted, punishment for evil deeds sometimes takes effect in this very life, and the Holy Qur'ān lays down the principle in clear words that every such punishment is a remedial measure:

> "And We did not send a prophet in a town but We overtook its people with distress and affliction in order that they might humble themselves" (7:94).

> "And certainly We sent apostles to nations before thee, then We seized them with distress and affliction in order that they might humble themselves" (6:42).

It is clear from this that God brings down His punishment upon a sinning people in order that they may turn to Him; in other words, that they may be awakened to the higher life. The same must, therefore, be the object of the punishment in hell. That this is really so is made clear, in the first place, by giving the utmost prominence to the quality of mercy in God, as already pointed out, and then by stating clearly that all men have been created for mercy: "Except those on whom thy Lord has mercy and for this did He create them" (11:119). The purpose of God must be ultimately fulfilled and, though man may bring down punishment on himself by his deeds, yet as God has created him for mercy, mercy is the ultimate end in the Divine scheme. Elsewhere we are told:

> And I have not created the jinn and the men except that they should serve Me (51:56).

They must, therefore, ultimately be made fit for the service of God, and that is the higher life. With all its fearfulness, hell is called a *maula* (friend) of the sinners, in one place (57:15), and their *umm* (mother), in another (101:9). Both these descriptions of hell are a clear indication that hell is meant only to purify a man of the dross which he has accumulated with his own hands, just as fire purifies gold of dross. In fact, it is to point to this truth that the Holy Qur'ān uses the word *fitna* (which originally means the *assaying of gold*, or *casting it into fire to purify it of dross*) both of the persecutions which the faithful are made to suffer (2:191, 29:2, 29:10) and of the punishment which the evil-doers shall suffer in hell (37:63), where the food which those in hell shall be given is called *fitna*, because the object in both cases is the same, the faithful being purified through persecutions and the evil-doers by hell-fire. Therefore hell is called a *friend* of the sinners, because, through suffering, it will make them fit for spiritual progress; and it is called a *mother* of the sinners to show that its connection with them is that of a mother with her child, the sinners being brought up as it were in the bosom of hell. The fire is a source of torment, but it is also a purifier. The keenness of the torments of the other life is due to the keener perception of the soul, which is the necessary result of its separation from the earthly vessel. Bliss and torment, therefore, grow equally keener in that life.

Punishment of Hell not everlasting.

It is in consonance with its remedial nature that we find it stated that the sinners shall ultimately be taken out of hell. It is true that the word *abad* is thrice used in the Holy Qur'ān in connection with the abiding in hell (4:169, 33:65, 72:23), but *abad* indicates *eternity* as well as *long time*, and that the latter significance must be taken in this case is made clear by the use, in the same connection, of the word *ahqab* (78:23), meaning *years* or *long years*. Besides this, a limitation is placed on the abiding in hell by the addition of the

words *except as thy Lord please*, the exception clearly indicating the
ultimate deliverance of those in hell. The following two verses may
be noted in this connection:

> He shall say, The fire is your abode, to abide in it, except as
> God please; for thy Lord is Knowing, Wise (6:128).

> So as to those who are unhappy, they shall be in the fire; for
> them shall be sighing and groaning in it: Abiding therein as
> long as the heavens and the earth endure, except as they
> Lord please; for thy Lord is the Mighty Doer of what He
> intends (11:106, 107).

Both these verses show clearly that the punishment of hell is not
everlasting. To make this conclusion clearer still, the latter of these
occasions may be compared with the next verse which describes the
abiding in paradise:

> And as to those who are made happy, they shall be in the
> garden, abiding in it as long as the heavens and the earth
> endure, except as thy Lord please: a gift never to be cut off
> (11:108).

The two expressions are similar; those in hell and those in paradise
abide in it as long as the heavens and the earth endure, with an
exception added in each case showing that they may be taken out of
it. The concluding statements are, however, different. In the case of
paradise, the idea that those in it may be taken out of it, if God
pleases, is immediately followed by the statement that it is a gift
which shall never be cut off, showing that they shall not be taken out
of paradise; while, in the case of hell, the idea of those in it being
taken out of it is confirmed by the concluding statement - "for thy
Lord is the mighty Doer of what He intends."

The conclusion drawn above is corroborated by the sayings of
the Holy Prophet. Thus a saying reported in the *Muslim* concludes:

> Then will God say, The angels and the prophets and the
> faithful have all in their turn interceded for the sinners, and
> now there remains none to intercede for them except the
> most Merciful of all merciful ones. So He will take out a

handful from fire and bring out a people who never worked any good.

Further, Bukhari records a saying to the effect that, when the sinners are taken out from hell, they shall be thrown into "the river of life," which clearly indicates that they shall be made fit for a higher life. The *Kanz al-'Ummāl* records the following: "Surely a day will come over hell when it will be like a field of corn that has dried up, after flourishing for a while"; "Surely a day will come over hell when there shall not be a single human in it." A saying of 'Umar is recorded as follows: "Even if the dwellers in hell may be numberless as the sands of the desert, a day will come when they will be taken out of it."

Hell is described by seven different names in the Holy Qur'ān, and these are supposed by some to be the seven divisions of hell. The most frequently occurring name is *jahannam*, which is like a proper name for *hell*. It is an Arabic word and the root-word means *great depth*. Next in frequency of occurrence is *jahīm*, which is derived from a root meaning the *intensity of fire*. Then comes *sa'īr*, from a root meaning the *kindling of fire*. Next to it is *saqar*, signifying *scorching heat*, which occurs only in two of the earliest chapters (54:48; 74:26, 27, 42). *Hutama*, which is derived from a root meaning *to crush*, occurs only twice in one early chapter (104:4, 5). *Lazā* (70:15), meaning a *flaming fire*, and *hāwiyah* (101:9), meaning *abyss*, or *a deep place of which the bottom cannot be reached*, occur once each.

Most frequently, however, the punishment of the evil-doers is spoken of as *nār*, meaning *fire*. It should be borne in mind that hell or the fire of hell is, according to the Holy Qur'ān, a manifestation of hidden realities (86:9). In other words, the spiritual torments and mental pangs that are often felt by an evil-doer in this very life assume a palpable shape in the life after death. "The fire kindled by God which rises above the hearts" (104:6, 7) becomes the flaming or intense or scorching fire of the next life. The *ahwā'* (low desires) of this life that are so often a hindrance in his awakening to a higher life and nobler deeds become the *hāwiyah* or *jahannam* (abysmal depth) to which the evil-doer makes himself to fall. Hence it is that intense

regret for the evil done is sometimes described as the fire: "Thus will
God show them their deeds to be intense regret to them, and they
shall not come forth from the fire" (2:167); and the day of
resurrection is accordingly called "the day of intense regret" (19:39).
Sometimes it is being debarred from the Divine presence that is
spoken of as a hell:

> Surely on that day they shall be debarred from their Lord;
> then surely they shall enter the burning fire (83:15, 16).

Sometimes disgrace is described as the punishment in the next life:
"Then on the resurrection day He will bring them to disgrace"
(16:27). It should also be noted that, as in paradise there is neither
sun, nor intense cold (76:13), so in hell there is both "boiling and
intensely cold water" (78:25); a "requital corresponding" to sin, it is
added, to show the real nature of the punishment.

Section 5
Revelation

Revelation, according to the Holy Qur'ān, is universal. Five kinds of revelation are referred to; revelation to inanimate objects, to animals lower than man, to men in general, to the prophets in particular, and to angels:

> On that day she (the earth) shall tell her news, as if thy Lord had revealed to he (99:4, 5).

> So He ordained them seven heavens in two periods and revealed in every heaven its affair (41:12).

> And thy Lord revealed to the bee, saying, Make hives in the mountains and in trees and in what they build: Then eat of all the fruits and walk in the ways of thy Lord submissively (16:68, 69).

> And We revealed to Moses' mother, saying, Give him suck, and when thou fearest for him cast him into the river and do not fear or grieve, for We will bring him back to thee and make him one of the apostles (28:7).

> And when I revealed to the disciples of (Jesus) saying, Believe in Me and My apostle (5:111).

> Surely We have revealed to thee as We revealed to Noah and the prophets after him (4:163).

> When thy Lord revealed to the angels, I am with you, so make firm those who believe (8:12).

The Divine revelation to each class is, however, of a different nature, and we are chiefly concerned with the Divine revelation to man. It is said to be of three kinds:

> And it is not for any mortal that God should speak to him except by inspiring or from behind a veil or by sending a

messenger and revealing by His permission what He pleases
(42:51).

The first of these, which is called *waḥy*, in the original, is the
inspiring of an idea into the heart, for the word *waḥy* is here used in
its literal significance of *a hasty suggestion*, as distinguished from
waḥy matluww, or revelation in words, which comes under the third
heading. The second mode of God's speaking to a man is said to be
from behind a veil, and this includes *ru'yā* (dream), *kashf* (vision),
and *ilhām* (when voices are heard or uttered in a state of trance. The
third kind, which is special to the prophets of God, is that in which
the angel (Gabrael) brings the Divine message in words. This is the
surest and clearest form of revelation, and such is the revelation of
the Qur'ān to the Holy Prophet. This is called *waḥy matluww*, or
revelation that is recited. The first two kinds of revelation may be
granted to prophets as well as to non-prophets, but the third is
granted only to the prophets, and is the highest form of revelation.

Thus, according to the Holy Qur'ān, revelation is a universal
fact, only the forms being different in the case of different recipients.
In fact, God speaks as He hears and sees. The revelation of the
prophets is, therefore, not the solitary experience of a certain class of
men; it is only the most developed form of revelation; in a less
developed form it is met with among all men, whether or not they are
believers in God. The Holy Qur'ān speaks of a vision of a king who
was apparently not a believer in God (12:43), and it had a deep
significance underlying it. Revelation, therefore, is the universal
experience of mankind, only the prophets receiving the highest form
of it.

Speaking of the first man, the Qur'ān has told us why revelation
from God was needed and what purpose it fulfilled. Man had two
objects before him: to conquer nature and to conquer self, to bring
under his control the powers of nature and his own desires. In the
allegorical story of Adam, related in 2:30-39, we are told that Adam
was given the knowledge of things, *i.e.* he was endowed with the
capacity to obtain knowledge of all things (2:31); he was also gifted
with the power to conquer nature, for the angels (beings controlling
the powers of nature) made obeisance to him (2:34); but Iblis (the

inciter of evil passions in man) did not make obeisance, and man fell a prey to his evil suggestions (2:36; 7:20-22). Man was powerful against all, but he was weak against himself, and he needed Divine help to give him sufficient strength to conquer his passions. This help came in the form of certain "words from His Lord" (2:37), *i.e.*, in Divine revelation which was granted to Adam; and as regards his posterity, the Divine law was given:

> There will come to you a guidance from Me; then whoever follows My guidance, no fear shall come upon them, nor shall they grieve. And as to those who disbelieve in and reject Our messages, they are the inmates of the fire; in it they shall abide (2:38, 39).

Revelation was thus needed to enable man to rise to higher stages of life; and in accordance with this Divine scheme, revelation was as much a need for one people as for another. God had endowed all men with the power to conquer nature; not one particular nation to the exclusion of others. He gave His physical sustenance to all men alike. Hence revelation which was needed for the moral and spiritual progress of man could not be given to one man or to one nation to the exclusion of others. Prophets were, therefore, sent to every nation, though it was not necessary that the names of all of them should have been mentioned in the Qur'ān:

> There is not a people but a warner has gone among them (35:24).

> And every nation had an apostle (10:47).

> And (We sent) apostles We have mentioned to thee before and apostles We have not mentioned to thee (4:164).

That is not all. Belief in the prophets of other nations is one of the fundamental principles of Islam. One of the three chief articles of faith of a Muslim, as stated at the commencement of the Holy Qur'ān is:

> And who believe in that which has been revealed to thee and that which was revealed before thee (2:4).

The Qur'ān thus lays down the basis of a brotherhood of the whole human race to which no other heavenly book has made any approach. That God is Lord of all the nations of the world is not here a dry dogma; it is a living principle, not only recognising that all nations were equally treated physically as well as spiritually, but going even further and making it an article of faith in Islam that we believe in all those prophets as we believe in the Prophet Muhammad. Surely a universal religion upon which the whole human race could agree could not go further than this.

The Arabic word for prophet is *nabī*, which is derived from *nab'*, meaning *an announcement of great utility*, also *a prophecy which gives information concerning the future*. The word *nabī* in its literal significance is applicable to anyone to whom prophecies about the future are revealed, but in the technical language of Islam it is applicable only to a man who is chosen by God to deliver His message to mankind. Such a person is also called a *rasūl* (*apostle*), which literally means *one sent*. The two words, *nabī* and *rasūl*, are interchangeable, but *rasūl* literally carries a wider significance, for the angels are also called *rusul* (messengers); see 35:1.

The prophet, according to the Holy Qur'ān, must be a human being, and hence it does not accept the doctrine of *incarnation*, or God in flesh. The reformation of man is entrusted to men to whom the Divine will is revealed, because only a man could serve as a model for men; even an angel could not have served that purpose. How could God in flesh serve as a model for frail human beings who have to meet hundreds of temptations, whereas for God there exists no possible temptation? Hence the Holy Qur'ān has affirmed in the clearest words that only prophets or men to whom God revealed His will could be sent as reformers:

> Had there been in the earth angels walking about as settlers, We would have sent down to them from heaven an angel as an apostle (17:95).

> And we did not send before them any but men to whom We sent revelation ... And We did not give them bodies not eating the food (21:7, 8).

To every prophet was given a book for the guidance of his
people:

> God raised prophets bearing good news and warning, and He
> revealed with them the book with truth that (the prophet)
> might judge between people in that in which they differed
> (2:213).

> Certainly We sent Our apostles with clear arguments and
> sent down with them the book and the measure (57:25).

The prophets were all sinless, both their words and their deeds
being in accordance with Divine commandments:

> And We did not send before thee any apostle but We
> revealed to him that there is no God but Me, therefore serve
> Me. And they say: The Beneficent God has taken to Himself
> a son; glory be to Him. Nay! they are honoured servants.
> They do not precede him in speech and only according to
> His commandment do they act (21:25-27).

> And it is not attributable to a prophet that he should act
> unfaithfully (3:161).

The revelation of the prophets is specially guarded:

> The Knower of the unseen — He does not reveal His secrets
> to any, except to him whom He chooses as an apostle; surely
> He makes a guard to march before him and after him, so that
> He may know that they have truly delivered the messages of
> their Lord (72:26-28).

The idea that the devil can insert suggestions into a prophet's
revelation is opposed to the above clear statement. 22:52 is
sometimes quoted in support of this idea, but that verse does not
speak of the *revelation* of prophets at all. It runs thus: "And We did
not send before thee any apostle or prophet but when he desired, the
devil made a suggestion respecting his desire." What is spoken of
here is not the prophet's revelation but his desire, *i.e.*, his desire to
establish the truth; and the devil here stands for the leaders of
wickedness, as it does in 2:14, the significance being that, when the

prophet desires to establish truth, the evil-doers make evil suggestions into the hearts of their followers to oppose him.

Chapter 3
Histories of Prophets
Section 1
Adam

It should be borne in mind in reading the histories of the prophets, as given in the Holy Qur'ān, that the object is not to narrate history as such, but to bring out certain characteristics of the histories of different nations, to mention incidents which contain prophetic allusion to the Holy Prophet's life, or to the future of Islam, and to comfort the Prophet with illustrations from previous sacred history that truth shall ultimately be established and that opposition shall entirely fail and be over-thrown. The Qur'ān does not concern itself with the details of those histories, not even with the details of what messages a prophet delivered to his people or how he was received. It contents itself with the broad facts that every prophet delivered the message of Unity, invited people to obey God and to do good to fellow-men, and aimed at the moral betterment of the people to whom he was sent. It shows, by mentioning prophets of Israelite and non-Israelite nationality, that the cardinal principles of the religion of all the prophets were one and the same. The references in the earlier chapters are very brief. Whatever details there are belong to a period when opposition to the Prophet was at its height and the object is, no doubt, to tell the opponents, when they were at the height of their power, that they could not escape their ultimate overthrow. Another point worth noting is that every prophet is spoken of as being sent to a single nation, with the exception of the Holy Prophet Muhammad, who is spoken of as being sent to all the nations of the world.

The Holy Qur'ān does not state when Adam was born or how he was born; it does not even state that he was the first man. The great Muslim divine, Muhammad ibn 'Ali al-Baqir, one of the twelve Shi'a Imams, is reported to have said that "millions of Adams passed away before our father Adam," and Ibn 'Arabi, the head of the Sufis, writes in his great work, the *Futūḥāt*, that forty thousand years before our Adam, there was another Adam. There is also a report accepted by the Imamiyya, according to which there were thirty Adams before our Adam, and this earth remained a waste after them for fifty thousand years; then it was inhabited for fifty thousand years; then was Adam created.

Again, the Holy Qur'ān does not say how Adam was made. It does not accept the Bible theory of his formation. It does say, indeed, that he was made from dust, but then it speaks of every son of man as being created from dust as well:

> O people! if you are in doubt about the raising (to life after death), then (know that) We have created you from dust, then from a small life-germ, then from a clot, then from a lump of flesh ... (22:5).

> He it is Who created you from dust, then from a small life-germ, then from a clot, then He brings you forth as a child (40:67).

> His companion said to him while disputing with him: Dost thou disbelieve in Him Who created thee from dust, then from a small life-germ, then He made thee a perfect man? (18:37).

Dust is the first stage of man's existence, and every man is made from it. How? The Holy Qur'ān itself explains:

> And certainly We created man of an extract of clay, then We made him a small life-germ in a firm resting-place (23:12, 13).

> And He began the creation of man from dust; then He made his progeny of an extract of water held in light estimation. Then He made him complete and breathed into him of His

spirit and made for you the ears and the eyes and the hearts (32:7-9).

Thus man's creation from dust means his creation from an extract of dust, an extract which eventually appears as a life-germ, because from the earth comes the food which through several processes assumes the form of the life-germ. It is noteworthy that the Holy Qur'ān here speaks of the spirit of God being breathed into *every* man, and the spirit in this case is not the animal soul, but the soul that enables a man to distinguish between right and wrong, the *nafs natiqa*, or the human soul or reason, and hence it is that the statement is immediately followed by the words, "and made for you ears and eyes and hearts."

Nor does the Qur'ān accept the Bible statement that Eve was made from a rib of Adam (Gen. 2:21, 22). It is no doubt stated in the Holy Book that God created people "from a single being and created its mate of the same" (4:1); but the meaning is evidently, *of the same kind* or *same essence*, for elsewhere we are told that mates or wives are created for all men from themselves — *anfus*, meaning *selves* or *kind*:

> And God has made for you wives from yourselves (16:72).

> And one of His signs is that He created mates for you from yourselves that you may incline to them, and He put between you love and compassion (30:21).

The devil's opposition to Adam, which is the chief characteristic of Adam's story, as given in the Holy Qur'ān, is mentioned in several different places, *i.e.*, four times in early Makka revelations (38:71-85; 17:61-65; 18:50; 20:116-124), twice in the later Makka revelations (15:26-44; 7:11-25), and once in early Madina revelation (2:30-39). To realise the true significance of the story, it is necessary to compare the various statements on the same or similar points. The first point is God's declaration of His will to create Adam or man:

> When thy Lord said to the angels: I am going to create a mortal from dust (38:71).

And when thy Lord said to the angels: I am going to create a mortal of the essence of black mud fashioned in shape (15:28).

And when thy Lord said to the angels: I am going to place in the earth one who shall rule in it (2:30).

Now on the first two occasions, it is simply a mortal whose creation is spoken of, while on the third occasion it is one who rules in the earth. The first two descriptions in their generality, and the third in particular, apply to all men and not to Adam alone, and hence the story of Adam is really the story of every man. Man's being a ruler refers to the high place he was intended to occupy on earth, ruling not only the animal creation but the very forces of nature, as the Qur'ān repeatedly states.

It is only on one occasion that attention is drawn to the darker side of the picture of humanity.

Wilt Thou place in it such as shall make mischief in it and shed blood? (2:30)

But the brighter side of that picture is presented in varying colours. In the earlier revelation we have:

When I have made him complete and breathed into him of My spirit (38:72, 15:29)

a description expressly applied to every human being in 32:9, but, later, man's vast capability to rule is pointed out in the words:

And He gave Adam knowledge of all the things (2:31)

a knowledge which is not given even to the angels (2:32). In knowledge really lies the power of man, and hence it is that the command to the angels to make obeisance to Adam follows immediately after the mention of his completion on the first two occasions and the giving of knowledge to him on the third.

This, as I have already stated, is the chief characteristic of Adam's story, the command to angels to make obeisance to Adam, showing that he is placed above even the angels, and that, below God, he occupies the highest place on earth. This is by virtue of his capacity for acquiring knowledge, and he acquires knowledge by slow degrees through his efforts; the light of the Divine spirit is within him, and by the use of that light he can rise to higher and higher eminences. Just as in the physical world, the acquirement of knowledge opens out before him new fields of advancement, so in the spiritual world the knowledge of things Divine opens out before him a higher life, a full manifestation of which begins with what is called the resurrection day. Hence we find that with the angels making obeisance to Adam on all seven occasions is mentioned the refusal of Iblis to submit. Now Iblis is the proper name of the devil, and in 18:50, he is plainly spoken of as being of the jinn or invisible beings of a lower order, in contrast with the angels or invisible beings of a higher order. These invisible beings are connected with the spiritual life of man, the angel urging him to good and the devil stirring up the baser passions in him and thus retarding his advancement to the higher life; see 50:21, where the impeller to evil or the devil is called a driver, and the caller to good or the angel is called a witness. Hence when it is stated that the devil refused to submit to Adam or man, it means that man's baser passions which the devil excites are really a hindrance to his progress, and that to attain to a higher life it is necessary that the devil should be made to submit or that the baser passions in man must be subdued. That such is the real significance was explained by the Holy Prophet himself when, on being questioned if he too had a devil as every other human being had, he replied in the affirmative, and added: "But God has helped me against him so that he is submissive." The devil and his progeny are, therefore, called man's enemy (18:50), with whom a man is required to carry on a struggle until the enemy submits to him.

The next point mentioned is that Adam and his wife are at first placed in a garden (20:117; 7:19; 2:35), a description of which is thus given in one place: "Thou shalt not be hungry therein nor bare of clothing;" "Thou shalt not be thirsty therein nor shalt thou feel the heat of the sun" (20:118, 119). Then we are told that Adam and his wife were told "to eat from it a plenteous food wherever you wish," but a warning was added: "Do not go near this tree for then you will be of the unjust" (2:35; 7:19). In order to tempt Adam, "the devil made an evil suggestion to them" (7:20; 20:120). It is noteworthy that in all the details of this story the Holy Qur'ān does not accept the Bible statements. It is not the serpent, "more subtle than any beast of the field," which comes and speaks to Eve and leads her astray, she in her turn leading man astray. It is the devil who makes an evil suggestion to Adam, or to both Adam and Eve, as he makes only evil suggestions to every son and daughter of Adam. By the devil's evil suggestion, man is made to think that the forbidden tree "is the tree of immortality and a kingdom which decays not" (20:120); and the suggestion is that God had "not forbidden you this tree except that you may not both become angels or that you may not become of the immortals" (7:20). Thus "he caused them to fall by deceit" (7:22), and they both ate of the tree. And what were the consequences? "They both ate of it, so their evil inclinations (or nakedness) became manifest to them, and they both began to cover themselves with leaves of the garden" (20:121; 7:22).

All this clearly shows that the garden is not an earthly garden, but stands for a state of contentment and rest in which there is no struggle. The tree which is not to be approached is always called "this tree" as if it had been just mentioned or as if it were a tree too well-known to need any description. This in itself gives an indication that it is the well-known *tree of evil*, for both good and evil are compared to two trees in 14:24, 25 and elsewhere. This is further corroborated by the devil's description of it as "the tree of immortality" (20:120), by which he deceived man (7:22), showing that it is really the tree which brings death, *i.e.*, the tree of evil. Another clue to the nature of this tree is afforded by 7:22 and 20:121, where the result of the eating of this tree is pointed out — "their evil inclinations became manifest to them". It is clearly the consciousness that man has done something wrong, something unworthy of himself. The attempt "to cover themselves with the leaves of the garden" (7:22; 20:121) is the desire to make up by human effort for the evil consequences of the fault committed. In fact, all this is placed beyond all doubt when the Qur'ān goes on to speak immediately afterwards of two kinds of clothing, the external clothing "to cover your nakedness and for beauty," and the spiritual clothing, "clothing that guards against evil, that is the best" (7:26); and in the same strain it goes on to generalize:

> O children of Adam! let not the devil cause you to fall into affliction as he expelled your parents from the garden, pulling off from them their clothing that he might show them their evil inclinations (or nakedness), for he sees you, he as well as his hosts, whence you cannot see them; indeed, We have made the devils to be the friends of those who do not believe (7:27).

The next verse then speaks of the indecencies committed by the unbelievers, and thus it becomes too clear to need further comment that it is of the tree of evil that the Holy Qur'ān speaks in *this tree*. When this is established, the conclusion is evident that the garden spoken of is a spiritual garden, the garden of contentment, as already pointed out. Its description as a garden where man feels no hunger (20:118), and at the same time eats from it a plenteous food (2:35), leads to the same conclusion. That the Qur'ān is here speaking allegorically of spiritual truths is also clear from 20:124:

> And whoever turns away from My reminder, his shall surely be a straitened life, and on the day of resurrection We will raise him blind.

The straitened life here clearly indicates the life spiritual. As a result of prompting man to evil, the devil, the inciter of the lower passions in man, is expelled from the garden for ever:

> Get out of it, for thou art driven away, and My curse is on thee to the day of judgment (38:77, 78; 15:34, 35).

Adam, who disobeys the Divine commandment through forgetfulness and not intentionally (20:115), is also expelled from the garden, but only for a while, to carry on a struggle with the devil that is his enemy:

> Go forth, some of you are enemies of others, and there is for you in the earth an abode and a provision for a time (2:36);

> Get forth you two therefrom — all — one of you enemy to another (20:123).

The state of struggle with the devil was destined to set man on the way to regain the garden. Man who is gifted with the power even to rule the angels and who could, therefore, make the devil to submit to himself, is expelled from the garden to make the necessary struggle and, through that struggle, helped by the Divine light of revelation, to regain the garden permanently, never more to be expelled from it. He turns to God and, finding help from that source of strength, conquers the devil:

> They said: Our Lord! we have been unjust to ourselves, and if Thou forgive us not and have not mercy on us, we shall certainly be of the losers (7:23).

> Then Adam received some words from his Lord, so He turned to him mercifully (2:37).

> Then his Lord chose him, so He turned to him mercifully and guided him (20:122).

If this is true of Adam in particular, it is also true of man generally. Communion with the Divine being obtained through His revelation brings man to a state in which the devil is for ever subdued, the state in which he has no more fear of the devil, nor does he commit evil to grieve over it:

> Surely there will come to you a guidance from Me, so whoever follows My guidance, no fear shall come upon them, nor shall they grieve (2:38).

> There will surely come to you guidance from Me, so whoever follows My guidance, he shall not go astray, nor be unhappy (20:123).

Anyone who considers carefully the details of this story, its manifestly allegorical nature, and the great purpose underlying it — that every man must carry on a struggle with his passions until he acquires the mastery over them — cannot for an instant entertain the idea that the Holy Qur'ān is in any way indebted to the Bible for the story of Adam.

Section 2

Noah

The most important point in connection with Noah's history, as related in the Holy Qur'ān, is that the deluge did not cover the whole face of the earth, nor did it bring about the destruction of all flesh on earth, as the Bible states (Gen. 7:21). The Qur'ān has laid stress on the point in the earliest revelation, speaking of Noah in ch. 71, which opens with the statement that "We sent Noah to his people," and ends with the statement that Noah's people rejected him and "because of their wrongs they were drowned" (71:25). All references to Noah lay stress on this point, *viz.*, that only Noah's people who opposed the truth, persecuted Noah, and planned against his life, were drowned. Thus:

> My Lord! my people give me the lie, therefore judge Thou between me and them with a just judgment and deliver me and those who are with me of the believers. So We delivered him and those with him in the laden ark. And We drowned the rest afterwards (26:117-120).

> And We helped him against the people who rejected Our communications; surely they were an evil people, so We drowned them all (21:77).

> And make the ark before Our eyes and according to Our revelation, and do not speak to Me in respect of those who are unjust, for they shall be drowned (11:37).

> But they rejected him, so We delivered him and those with him in the ark, and We made them rulers and drowned those who rejected Our communications (10:73; 7:64).

The only details of any importance about Noah are contained in the 11th chapter, which speaks of the making of an ark, Noah's embarking on it, and how it ultimately rested on the Judi, one of the mountains which divide Armenia on the south from Mesopotamia, and adds an incident about a son of Noah who was also drowned because he was "the doer of other than good deeds" (11:46). A very short notice of him, contained in 29:14, 15, adds that he remained among his people for 950 years, which may refer either to his own span of life or to the duration of his law. In 66:10, his wife is mentioned along with Lot's wife as having acted treacherously towards him.

Section 3
Non-Biblical Prophets

The history of Noah in the Holy Qur'ān is generally followed, when a chronological order is observed, by the history of the prophet Hūd, who was sent to the tribe of 'Ād. This tribe lived in the desert of al-Aḥqāf (46:21), extending from Oman to Hadzramaut, in the south of Arabia. The tribe takes its name from 'Ād, the grandson of Aram, the grandson of Noah, and is sometimes called the first 'Ād (53:50) as distinguished from the tribe of Thamūd, which is called the second 'Ād. It was a powerful tribe, as the inscriptions now discovered show, and probably had spread far and wide. The prophet Hūd is not mentioned in the Bible, nor is the prophet Ṣāliḥ who was sent to the tribe of Thamūd, which is often mentioned along with 'Ād, though territorially separated from it. Thamūd lived in al-Ḥijr (15:80) to the north of Madina. The only important things mentioned about 'Ād are that they were successors of Noah's people (7:69), that they made lofty buildings (the words thus translated may also signify that they were men of tall statures), being the most powerful nation of their day (89:7, 8), and that they were destroyed by a strong wind (69:6, 7; 54:19). About Thamūd we are told that they hewed out houses in the mountains (7:74), traces of these rock habitations being still met with in the Holy Prophet's time (27:52), and that they were destroyed by an earthquake (7:78). There is mention of a she-camel which was given to them as a sign, they being warned that if they slew the she-camel, punishment would overtake them. The many legends about this she-camel are not met with in the Qur'ān, and the facts seem to be that they had laid a plan for the murder of their prophet (27:48, 49) and the slaying of the she-camel was a sign that they were about to execute their final plan.

These are not the only prophets mentioned in the Qur'ān about whom the Bible is silent. The Qur'ān speaks of a prophet of the name of Luqmān (31:13) who seems to have been an Ethiopian. His teachings are quoted as specially laying stress on humility and meekness (31:17-19). It also speaks of a non-Israelite prophet who was contemporaneous with Moses and to whom Moses went in search of knowledge (18:60-82). He lived at the junction of the two Niles (18:60), *i.e.*, at Khartoom. Again it speaks of Darius I, a king of Persia, who is called _Dhul-qarnain_, or *the two-horned one*, on the basis of Daniel's vision (Dan. 8:20), and what is stated of him shows that he is also looked upon as the prophet of a nation. All this is quite in accordance with the clear doctrine laid down in the Holy Qur'ān that a prophet was sent to every nation.

Section 4
Abraham

Abraham and Moses are the two prophets whose histories are given the greatest prominence in the Holy Qur'ān, Abraham being spoken of nearly 70 times and Moses over 130 times. The importance of Abraham was due to his acceptance by all the three different communities that resided in Arabia, the Jews, the Christians, and the idolaters; he was thus in a way the link which united them, notwithstanding the divergence of their religious views. It is for this reason that they are again and again invited to the religion of Abraham:

> And they say: Be Jews or Christians, you will be on the right course. Say: Nay, the religion of Abraham, the upright one, and he was not one of the polytheists (2:135).

> And who has a better religion than he who submits himself entirely to God, and he is the doer of good to others and follows the faith of Abraham, the upright one (4:125).

> Say: Surely my Lord has guided me to the right path, to a most right religion, the faith of Abraham, the upright one, and he was not of the polytheists (6:161).

Notwithstanding that the righteousness of Abraham was an established fact with these three communities, Abraham's religion was not the religion of any of them:

> Abraham was not a Jew or a Christian, but he was an upright man, a Muslim, and he was not one of the polytheists (3:67).

The three communities are, in fact, told to find out the common element of the three religions, for only that could be the religion of Abraham. This common element was belief in the existence of the One Supreme God. The word *hanīf*, which I have translated *upright*, is most frequently used in connection with Abraham. The root-word *ḥanf* means *inclining*, or *declining*, and hence *ḥanīf* means *one inclining to a right state* according to Raghib, the best authority on the lexicology of the Holy Qur'ān. Wherever used, it seems to indicate a firmness in adhering to the right state as opposed to an inclining to polytheism on the part of the Jews and the Christians. Abraham appears in the Holy Qur'ān as the most forceful preacher against idolatry and polytheism of every kind, and his zeal to rid humanity of this grossest of superstitions gives us really a picture of the Holy Prophet's mind. In fact, every prophet in the Holy Qur'ān represents a particular phase of the character of the Holy Prophet Muhammad, and Abraham stands for the iconoclastic tendency on the one hand and entire submission to God on the other. His preaching against idolatry is referred to in 6:74; 19:42-48; 21:52-65; 26:69-84; 29:16, 17; 37:85-96; 43:26, 27. He also preaches against the worship of heavenly bodies (see 6:75-83; 37:88, 89); but he went a step further and broke the idols, and this he did after he had plainly told his people that he would make clear to them the helplessness of their supposed deities:

> And by God! I will certainly strive against your idols after you go away, turning back. So he broke them into pieces except the chief of them that haply they might return to it (21:57, 58).

The same incident is also referred to earlier, in 37:91-96, where he is spoken of as having broken them secretly, *i.e.*, in the absence of their worshippers. This breaking of the idols by Abraham was no doubt a prophecy that the idols which then polluted the House sanctified by Abraham would ultimately be broken by the Holy Prophet, and so it happened after the conquest of Makka. Abraham's zeal for the establishment of the Unity of God is also displayed by his leaving enduring traditions among the Arabs that he was a preacher of Unity: "And he made it a word to continue in his posterity that they may return" (43:28), where *it* refers to the worship of One God.

The second phase of Abraham's character in which he represents the Holy Prophet is his entire submission to God. Though every prophet undoubtedly submitted to God, yet particular stress is laid upon Abraham's submission (see 2:124, 131; 3:67; 4:125; 16:120; 37:83, 84). His submission to God was so perfect that, when he received a commandment to sacrifice his only son Ishmael, he did not hesitate a minute, though "when they both submitted and he threw him down upon his forehead," the voice of God came to him that he had "shown the truth of the vision" (37:103-105), in obedience to which he was going to sacrifice his son, and that the sacrifice of a ram should commemorate the occasion (37:107) as a sign that the animal in man was to be sacrificed to the divine in him. Thus the incident affords an illustration of the complete submission of Abraham to God and contains, no doubt, a prophetic reference to the complete submission of the Holy Prophet Muhammad and his followers, who showed their willingness to lay down their own lives and the lives of those dearest to them to defend the truth. It may also be remarked here that, according to the Holy Qur'ān, Ishmael was the son whom Abraham was ordered to sacrifice, as it speaks of the good news of Isaac's birth being given to Abraham after the incident of the sacrifice (37:112). This contradicts the Bible statement, which speaks of Isaac as being the son who was ordered to be sacrificed; but the Bible contradicts itself when it says: "Take now thy son, thine only son Isaac" (Gen. 22:2). He is called "thine only son" in vv. 12 and 16. Now Isaac could not, by any stretch of imagination be called an "only son", as Ishmael was much older than Isaac. Only Ishmael could be called an only son before Isaac's birth, and, therefore, the text has no doubt been altered in favour of Isaac. Moreover, both the Bible and the Holy Qur'ān agree that a ram was sacrificed instead of the lad, but the sacrifice of a ram is commemorated among Ishmael's descendants, not among Isaac's, and this is additional testimony to the truth of what the Qur'ān states.

Another important point relating to Abraham is his connection and that of Ishmael with the Ka'ba, the sacred house at Makka. The Qur'ān does not leave the least doubt about it. It was there that Abraham had left Ishmael, not in the wilderness of Beershaba, as Abraham's prayer referred to in the Holy Qur'ān shows:

> O our Lord! I have settled a part of my offspring in a valley
> unproductive of fruit near Thy Sacred House, our Lord! that
> they may keep up prayer (14:37).

From this, as also from a saying of the Holy Prophet, it further
appears that Abraham had left Ishmael in Arabia in accordance with
a Divine commandment, not at the instigation of his wife Sarah, as
the Bible would have it (Gen. 21:10). In fact, it was all done in
accordance with a Divine scheme so that "the stone which the
builders rejected" should become "the head of the corner" (Matt.
21:42; Ps. 118:22). Ishmael was that stone for, whereas from the
descendants of Israel, came numerous prophets, from the descendants
of him who was cast into the wilderness, and whom the Israelites
began to hate though he was their brother, came the last of the
prophets who became the head of the corner. The strong connection
of Abraham and Ishmael with the Ka'ba is thus voiced in the Holy
Qur'ān:

> When Abraham and Ishmael raised the foundations of the
> House: Our Lord! accept from us (2:127).

From this it appears that Abraham and Ishmael rebuilt the Ka'ba.
That it was there already is shown by 14:37, as also by 3:96, which
calls it "the first house appointed for men." Abraham is also stated
to have prayed for Makka to be made the spiritual centre of the
world:

> My Lord! make this city secure and save me and my sons
> from worshipping idols (14:35; 2:126).

Moreover, Abraham and Ishmael prayed for the raising up of a
prophet from among their descendants:

> Our Lord! and make us both submissive to Thee and raise
> from our offspring a nation submitting to Thee and show us
> our ways of devotion and turn to us mercifully, for Thou art
> the Oft-returning to mercy, the Merciful. Our Lord! and raise
> up in them an apostle from among them who should recite
> to them Thy communications and teach them the Book and
> the wisdom, and purify them, for Thou art the Mighty, the
> Wise (2:128, 129).

It is in reference to this prayer that the Holy Prophet is reported to have said: "I am the prayer of my father Abraham." The prayer for "a nation submitting to Thee", or a Muslim nation, as contained in 2:128, was clearly prophetical at the time of its revelation, for the circumstances then were against such a nation coming into existence, and the few scattered Muslims, against overwhelming numbers of opponents who were bent upon their extermination, could not be called a *nation*.

Another trait of Abraham's character in which he represents the Holy Prophet is that he was very lenient towards his foes, so much so that he pleaded for Lot's people to be saved, though he knew that they were transgressors (11:74-76), and his prayer contains the memorable words:

> Whoever follows me, he is surely of me; and whoever disobeys me — Thou surely art Forgiving, Merciful (14:36)

and this notwithstanding that he had to sever connection with those opponents:

> We are clear of you and of what you serve besides God; we declare ourselves to be clear of you, and enmity and hatred have appeared between us and you forever until you believe in God alone (60:4).

Exactly in the same manner was the Holy Prophet compelled to sever his connection with the unbelievers, yet, in his hour of triumph, when all those enemies who had left no stone unturned to annihilate the Muslims were at his mercy, he forgave them all.

Section 5
Moses

Moses is the most frequently mentioned of all the prophets spoken of in the Holy Qur'ān, and the details of his life are dwelt upon to a much greater extent than are the details of any other prophet's life. He is, moreover, the prophet to whom reference is made earliest in the Holy Book, in the chapter entitled *al-Muzzammil*, which stands third in the chronological order. Here it is that the reason is also met with for giving so much importance to his history:

> "We have sent to you an apostle, a bearer of witness to you, as We sent an apostle to Pharaoh" (73:15).

This verse points out the likeness of the Holy Prophet Muhammad to Moses, a likeness which Moses himself had pointed out in Deut. 18:15, 18:

> "Thy Lord thy God will raise up unto thee a Prophet from the midst of thee, of thy brethren, like unto me; unto him ye shall hearken ... I will raise them up a prophet from among their brethren like unto thee, and will put My words in his mouth."

We are told twice that the promised prophet, the like of Moses, shall appear from among "their brethren." The people addressed here are the Israelites, and, therefore, "their brethren" could mean only the Ishmaelites. Actually no Israelite prophet ever claimed to be the like of Moses. Up to the time of Jesus Christ, we find the Israelites still awaiting the advent of the promised "like" of Moses, for John the Baptist was asked if he was Christ or Elias or *that Prophet* (Revised Version, *the Prophet*), the reference in the margin being given to Deut. 18:15, 18. Nor did Jesus Christ ever say that he was the like of Moses, and his apostles still awaited the fulfilment of that prophecy after Jesus' crucifixion:

For Moses truly said unto the fathers, A prophet shall the Lord your God raise up unto you of your brethren, like unto me (Acts 3:22).

It was only the revelation of the Holy Prophet, and that the earliest, which pointed out the fulfilment of the prophecy of Deut. 18:15, 18 in the advent of a Prophet like Moses. This claim is made still plainer in a later revelation:

Have you considered if it is from God, and you disbelieve in it, and a witness from among the children of Israel has borne witness of one like him (46:10).

The history of Moses begins with a revelation to his mother to cast the child into the river, where he is picked up by Pharaoh's people (20:38, 39; 28:7, 8), and brought up by Pharaoh (26:18). When grown up, he finds one day an Israelite being oppressed by an Egyptian and strikes the Egyptian with his fist in order to save the Israelite. The Egyptian is accidentally killed, and Moses, on being informed that he cannot expect any justice from the authorities, flies to Midian (28:14-21). There he meets Jethro, marries his daughter and, after ten years, goes back to Egypt (28:22-29).

On his way back, he is called to the office of a prophet (19:52; 20:11-14; 27:8, 9; 28:30; 79:15, 16), and sees in a visionary state that his staff has become a serpent and his hand is white (20:17-23; 27:10-12; 28:31, 32). He is commanded to go to Pharaoh and to demand the deliverance of the Israelites (7:103-105; 20:46-48; 26:15-17; 44:18). He asks for a helper, Aaron, his brother (20:25-35; 26:12-14; 28:33, 34). Pharaoh has a discussion with him (20:47-55; 26:18, 31). A secret believer from among Pharaoh's people argues on behalf of Moses (40:28-45). Pharaoh demands signs, and the two signs of the staff and the hand are shown (7:107, 108; 26:32, 33; 79:20). Pharaoh calls to his aid the enchanters, whose tricks do not avail aught against Moses (7:113-126; 10:80-82; 20:60-73; 26:38-51), and they believe in him (7:120, 121; 20: 70; 26:46-48). Moses then shows other signs (7:130, 133), nine in all (17:101). Every time that distress befalls Pharaoh, he requests Moses to pray for its removal, promising to believe when it was removed, but fails to keep his promise (7:134, 135; 43:49, 50). Moses exhorts his people to patience and prayer (7:128; 10:84). He is ultimately commanded to leave Egypt and crosses the sea, while Pharaoh and his hosts are drowned (2:50; 7:138; 10:90; 20:78; 26:53-66).

He then retires to the mountain for forty days to receive the law (2:51; 7:143-145; 20: 83, 84), and the Israelite leaders with him demand that God should be shown to them manifestly (2:55). Moses prays to God that He may show Himself to him (7:143). A severe earthquake overtakes Moses and his companions (7:143, 155), and they fall down in a state of swoon. Moses recovers (7:143) and prays for his companions (7:155), who are restored to their senses (2:55, 56). Moses is given the Torah (7:142-145), the book being revealed to him (2:53; 6:91) as books were revealed to other prophets. On his return, he finds his people worshipping the image of a calf which they had made in his absence under the directions of one called a Samiri (2:51; 7:150; 20:86-89). Aaron had warned them of their error before the coming of Moses, but they did not give it up (20:90, 91). The image is burned and the ashes are scattered in the sea (20:97). Moses orders his people to slaughter a cow, which they were unwilling to do, and obeyed the order after much hesitation (2:67-71). His own people make false imputations against him (33:69; 61:5). He asks his people to march on the Holy Land, but they refuse, and are made to wander in the wilderness for forty years (5:21-26).

I have given some of the more important details of Moses' life. Many other details are met with which the reader can see for himself. It would be noted that there are here some very important differences from the Bible narrative; for instance, Moses is not shown to be guilty of the murder of the Egyptian, his death being only accidental; nor is Aaron guilty of making or helping to make the calf. The importance attached to his life-story is due to his likeness to the Holy Prophet Muhammad. Moses was both a law-giver and a nation-builder, and so was the Holy Prophet Muhammad to be. These two characteristics are not to be met with in any other Israelite prophet, and it will be seen that the details given above, as well as the other details met with about Moses in the Holy Qur'ān, relate to one or other of these two characteristics, more to the latter than to the former. In both these capacities, as a law-giver and as a nation-builder, the Holy Prophet Muhammad had to work on an immensely wider scale than did Moses. The law of Moses was meant for a particular race, the Israelites, and even among them prophets appeared after Moses to meet the new needs and to effect the necessary alterations and abrogations; but the law given to the Holy Prophet Muhammad was meant for the whole human race and was made perfect, as he was the Prophet for all nations and for all times, no prophet appearing after him. This difference is repeatedly brought out in the Holy Qur'ān; the following quotations serve only as an example:

> And We gave the book to Moses, so be not in doubt concerning the receiving of it, and We made it a guide for the children of Israel (32:23).

> Blessed is He who sent down the Furqan upon His servant that he may be a warner to the nations (25:1).

> And it is naught but a reminder to the nations (68:52).

> This day have I perfected for you your religion and completed My favour on you (5:3).

Though the law is made perfect in the Holy Qur'ān and no prophet appears after the Holy Prophet Muhammad, yet, to meet new needs, the door is always open to work out the principles enunciated in the Holy Book and to deduce new laws for them to meet the requirements of the times.

As a nation-builder, the work of Moses occupies a very prominent place in his own life-story as well as in the history of the world. It was the first message with which he was entrusted:

> Go to Pharaoh and say, We are the messengers of the Lord of the worlds that send with us the children of Israel (26:16, 17).

The law was given to him long afterwards. The work was no doubt one of the greatest difficulty, for the Israelites had been in a state of slavery to the Pharaohs of Egypt for about four centuries. But great and important as was Moses' work, his message was very limited in comparison with the message with which the Holy Prophet Muhammad was entrusted. He had to build a nation on quite a new principle, a nation not united by any ties of blood, race, colour, or country, but united by a moral and spiritual outlook, united by a belief in the Unity of God and in His all-pervading Lordship. Such was to be the Muslim nation in which the Arab and the non-Arab, the white and the black, the Semitic and the Aryan, were all to be on one level. The whole world was the country and the whole of humanity the race, out of which this nation was to be formed. With this apparently impossible task the Prophet was entrusted and, single-handed, in the face of all difficulties, he built up the foundations of the new nation within the short period of twenty years. Such a huge task cannot be placed to the credit of any other man in the history of the world.

Section 6
Jesus Christ

Jesus Christ is mentioned by three different names: *'Īsā* (Jesus), *Ibn Maryam* (the son of Mary), and *al-Masīḥ* (the Messiah). 'Īsā, or Jesus, is the proper name; he is called the son of Mary to show that, like every human child, he was born of a woman, and one born of a woman could not be God (Job 25:4); and he is called the Messiah because he held the office of a prophet among the Israelites. But *masīḥ* also means *one who travels in the land*, and the title may have reference to his travels from one country to another.

Jesus Christ is mentioned only some thirty-five times in the Holy Qur'ān, and the longest notices of him which speak of his birth and mission are those in which he is mentioned along with John the Baptist. These occur in ch. 19, which receives the name of Mary, his mother, and is one of the early Makka revelations, and in ch. 3, which receives the name of the Family of 'Imrān, and is one of the early Madina revelations. Besides these two occasions where the life-story of Jesus Christ is dealt with at some length, along with the Christian doctrine, there is another early Makka revelation, the 18th chapter, which deals with the history of Christianity, and the 5th chapter, a late Madina revelation, which deals at length with the Christian violation of the covenant. Another important fact in connection with the mention of Jesus Christ is that, though the same importance is not given to his life-story as to that of Moses, yet much importance is attached to a refutation of the erroneous doctrines connected with his name, a refutation starting with one of the earliest revelations in ch. 112 and continuing up to the latest in ch. 9.

As regards the life-story of Jesus Christ, the earliest revelation is ch. 19, which opens with the prayer of Zacharias for a son, and the first section deals with the birth and mission of John. The second section deals with the birth and mission of Jesus Christ. V. 16 states that Mary, who lived in the holy temple as a child (3:37), had to leave the precincts of the temple for an eastern place, probably Nazareth. This no doubt took place on her attaining puberty, for the Jews considered a woman to be impure during her monthly courses. There she received in a vision the news of the birth of a son (v. 19). She wonders, because she had not as yet been married (v. 20), and is told that the child to whom she would give birth would be made a guide for the people, "a sign to men and a mercy from Us" (v. 21). We are then told that she conceived him (v. 22), "as women conceive", according to a saying of the Holy Prophet. After this she had to go to a distant place (compare Luke 2:2-6), and her confinement came during the journey (vv. 22, 23).

The third chapter, *the Family of 'Imrān*, gives some details on these points not to be met with in ch. 19. In the first place, it speaks of the birth of Mary herself, who, according to a vow made by her mother, was to be devoted to the service of the temple at Jerusalem (3:35). Notwithstanding this, she prays, when she gives birth to the child, that both the girl and "her offspring" may be vouchsafed Divine protection as against the devil (3:36), showing that her mother expected her to marry and bear children as women do. V. 37 tells us that, as a child, she remained in the charge of Zacharias and was brought up as a devout child. Here the subject is changed, Zacharias praying for and being granted a son, John the Baptist. The original subject is reverted to in v. 42, where Mary is spoken of as being chosen above other women of her time. Evidently this refers to the time when she was quite a grown-up girl, and then, in v. 44, we are again told that there was a contention as to the man in whose charge Mary should be placed. This in all probability refers to arrangements for her marriage, for her charge as a child has already been spoken of clearly, in 3:37. It is at this point that the earlier narrative in ch. 19 begins speaking of her leaving the precincts of the temple for an eastern place. The part common to both narratives is her receiving the news in a vision, the angels speaking to her according to 3:45, that she would give birth to a son, who would come in fulfilment of the Messianic prophecy. The next verse tells us that he would attain to old age and be one of the righteous. In 3:47 she wonders, because her marriage had not as yet taken place, and is re-assured. The further details of conception and birth are not met with here.

In both narratives, however, there is a gap up to the time that Jesus is called and preaches to his people. In ch. 3, the news of the birth of a son in v. 47 is immediately followed in vv. 48 and 49 by the call of Jesus and his preaching. In ch. 19, the account of his birth is similarly followed. Evidently the coming of Mary with Jesus to her people, as spoken of in 19:27, does not relate to the time of the birth, which is the subject-matter of the previous verse, but to a later time, because it is unthinkable that a woman should thus make a show of a newborn baby, and because Mary at the time was journeying to a distant place (19:22). V. 27 speaking of Mary going along with Jesus to her people while he was riding an animal, probably contains a reference to the episode of Jesus riding on an ass and a colt (Matt. 21:1-7). Moreover, the reply given by Jesus Christ to the people on this occasion cannot possibly relate to the time when he was a mere baby, because in that reply he clearly speaks of *having been made* a prophet and *having been commanded* to say prayers and give alms while *he lived*. A baby a day old could not have been made a prophet, nor could he be commanded to say prayers and give alms. Here are the words, conclusively showing that 19:30-32 relates to the time when Jesus had received the call, and offended the elders of the Israelites by his preaching:

> He said: I am a servant of God; He has given me the Book and made me a prophet, and He has made me blessed wherever I may be, and He has enjoined on me prayer and poor-rate as long as I live, and dutiful to my mother, and He has not made me insolent, unblessed.

As I have said, however, greater stress is laid upon the doctrines connected with the name of Jesus than upon the details of his life, and even the circumstances relating to his life are meant to be a denial of his divinity. We are told that his mother conceived him, quite a superfluous detail of life-history unless it is meant to show that he could not be God or the son of God, for the idea of conception in the mother's womb is incompatible with Divinity. The severity of pains during labour, which makes Mary utter: "O, would

that I had died before this" (19:23), is not only to show that Mary
gave birth to Jesus in the ordinary circumstances which women
experience in giving birth to children, but also seems to contain a
deeper reference to Gen. 3:16, "In sorrow thou shalt bring forth
children," which, according to the Bible, was the punishment
inflicted on woman because of Eve's alleged sin. He is also
mentioned as speaking "when in the cradle and when of old age"
(3:46), to show the change of condition from childhood to old age,
while change in the Divine Being is impossible. The prominent
features of his preaching when called to the office of a prophet also
show the same tendency. He is spoken of as "a servant of God"
(19:30; 43:59), by no means disdaining to be a servant of God
(4:172), as "a prophet" (19:30), "an apostle to the children of Israel"
(3:49), nothing more than an apostle before whom numerous apostles
had passed away (5:75), one who had to learn "the Torah" (3:48),
repeatedly saying: "God is my Lord and your Lord; therefore serve
Him" (3:51; 5:117; 19:36; 43:64). along with his mother, he is
spoken of as "eating food" (5:75), showing that he had all the needs
and weaknesses of a mortal. He is even made to deny his divinity in
plain words:

> And when God will say, O Jesus, son of Mary! didst thou
> say to men, Take me and my mother for two gods besides
> God; he will say, Glory be to Thee, it did not befit me that
> I should say what I had no right to say (5:116).

A noteworthy feature of the narrative of Jesus Christ in the Holy
Qur'ān is the mention of his death which occurs thrice in plain words
and several times by implication:

> When God said, O Jesus! I will cause thee to die and exalt
> thee in My presence and clear thee of those who disbelieve,
> and make those who follow thee above those who disbelieve
> to the day of resurrection (3:55).

> I did not say to them aught save what Thou didst enjoin me
> with, that serve God, my Lord and your Lord, and I was a
> witness of them so long as I was among them, but when

Thou didst cause me to die, Thou wert the watcher over them, and Thou art witness of all things (5:117).

Certainly they disbelieve who say that God - He is the Messiah, son of Mary. Say: Who then could control anything as against God when He wished to destroy the Messiah son of Mary and his mother and all those on earth (5:17).

The first of these verses shows that Jesus Christ was comforted by Divine revelation, when his enemies planned to take away his life by violence, that he would be made to die a natural death; but this promise does not stand alone; it is the first of four promises: death, after death exaltation in the Divine presence, then clearance from false charges, and lastly the triumph of the Christians over the Jews. The order in which these promises are mentioned is the order in which they actually took place. The second verse shows that the doctrine of the Divinity of Jesus Christ did not grow up before his eyes, but was invented by his followers *after* his death, and the verse is conclusive as showing that Jesus Christ was made a god after his death. The third reason gives the reason for laying stress on his death, and says in effect that, if Jesus Christ had been God, as alleged by the Christians, he would not have tasted of death, as did his mother and his compatriots.

Of the verses which speak of Jesus Christ's death by implication, I would content myself with only three:

The Messiah, son of Mary, is no more than an apostle, the apostles before him have indeed passed away; and his mother was a truthful woman; they both used to eat food; see how We make the communications clear to them, then behold how they are turned away (5:75).

And Muhammad is no more than an apostle; the apostles before him have indeed passed away (3:144).

And those whom they call on besides God have not created anything while they are themselves created; dead are they, not living, and they know not when they shall be raised (16:20, 21).

The first verse in this case states that, as all the apostles before Jesus Christ had died, so he, too, must have died, because like them he was a mortal and like them he ate food. The second states clearly that all the prophets before Muhammad had passed away and thus includes Jesus Christ among the dead. The third says that all those who had been taken as gods before the Qur'ān — and Jesus Christ was one of them — were dead, not one of them being alive. Yet, in spite of so many clear statements, the idea finds acceptance among the Muslims that Jesus Christ is still alive. This idea no doubt came originally from the Christian tradition, and then, owing to the prophecy of a second advent of the Messiah, which meant nothing more nor less than the appearance of one in his "spirit and power" (Luke 1:17), it slowly gained ground. There is nothing, however, in the Holy Qur'ān, or even in the sayings of the Holy Prophet, which lends any support to this idea. True it is that the Holy Qur'ān speaks of the *raf*, or exaltation, of Jesus Christ, but it is after his death, as plainly stated in 3:55. Nor does *raf* (exaltation) by God signify a translation of the body of a mortal to heaven; it signifies only exaltation in rank.

One point, however, needs to be elucidated. The Holy Qur'ān negatives the death of Jesus on the cross, but a negation of death by crucifixion does not amount to a negation of natural death. What actually happened is stated thus:

> And they did not kill him, nor did they cause his death by crucifixion, but he was made to appear to them like (one crucified), and those who differ therein are only in a doubt about it (4:157).

The Qur'ān thus asserts that Jesus Christ did not meet with his death on the cross, but was made to resemble one crucified. The story that he was lifted up to heaven while someone else was made to resemble him and suffered crucifixion is one of which no trace is met with in the Holy Book, nor in any saying of the Holy Prophet. What the Qur'ān says concerning the crucifixion of Jesus — that he was nailed to the cross but did not die on it — is exactly what appears to be the truth from a perusal of the Gospels. The Qur'ān is not a book of history and is not concerned with the details of what happened to him after the crucifixion, but it tells us that both he and his mother were given "a shelter on a lofty ground having meadows and springs" (23:50), which description applies to Kashmir; and there is a saying of the Holy Prophet that Jesus lived to the age of 120 years.

Thus, according to the Qur'ān, Jesus Christ was born like a mortal and he died like a mortal. He lived the life of a righteous man and was entrusted with a Divine message "to the Israelites" (3:49), but these people rejected him, planned against his life, and denounced him as a bastard, calling his mother an adultress (4:156). If the Qur'ān had, therefore, to denounce the doctrine of his divinity it had also to defend him against false accusations. It is for this reason that it speaks of his mother as "a truthful woman" (5:75), and speaks of Jesus Christ himself as "a word" from God and "a spirit from Him." He is called *a word from God* because he came in fulfilment of a word "which He communicated to Mary" (4:171), just as the Holy Prophet is reported to have said, "I am the prayer of my father, Abraham," because of the prayer of Abraham, referred to in 2:129. Mary was told that the son she would bear would be a righteous man and a prophet, and it is in reference to this prophecy that he is called *a word from God*. Or, it may be in reference to the prophecies of the previous prophets, that he may have been so called. Similarly, his being called a spirit from Him may be in reference to the denial of the charge of illegitimacy against him, because illicit sexual relations are ascribed to the devil. It must, however, be borne in mind that Jesus is spoken of only as *a* word from God or *a* spirit from Him, and not as *the* word or *the* spirit. Though he may have been called *a word* especially with reference to the prophecy of his birth, yet every creature of God is His word in one sense, because it comes into existence by a Divine commandment, and hence it is that the Holy Qur'ān speaks of the words of God as being too numerous to be exhausted by writing down:

> Say, If the sea were ink for the words of my Lord, the sea would be consumed before the words of my Lord are exhausted, though We were to bring the like of that sea to add thereto (18:109).

Similarly, though he may have been called a spirit from God in reference to the charge against his mother, the Holy Qur'ān also speaks of the spirit of God being breathed into every human being:

> Then He made his progeny of an extract, of water held in light estimation. Then He made him complete and breathed into him of His spiri (32:8, 9).

This mention of the spirit of God being breathed into every man seems to be directed against the Christian doctrine that every man is born in sin and a bond-slave to the devil.

Section 7
Other Bible Prophets

Of the other Bible prophets mentioned in the Holy Qur'ān, Enoch, who appeared before Noah, is mentioned twice under the name of Idrīs (19:56; 21:85). His being raised to an elevated state (19:57) has been misconstrued to mean his being raised alive to heaven, and here, too, the influence of Christian tradition has been at work. Gen. 5:24 says that "Enoch walked with God, and he was not, for God took him," but Paul goes a step further and says: "By faith Enoch was translated that he should not see death: and was not found because God had translated him" (Heb. 11:5). Reliable commentators have, however, held that what is stated about Enoch in the Qur'ān as being "raised to an elevated state" signifies only his exaltation to the rank of prophethood, and not his translation to upper regions.

Lot is mentioned along with Abraham because he was contemporaneous with him and was also his nephew; see 11:69-83; 15:51-76; 29:16-26, 31-35; 51:24-37. Some Christian writers have found fault with the Qur'ān in recognising him as one of the prophets. Nevertheless, Gen. 19:30-38, which speaks of his incestuous intercourse in a state of intoxication with his daughters, is quite inconsistent even with his righteousness, which is asserted in Gen. 18:23. In 2 Pet. 2:7, 8, he is called "just Lot" whose "righteous soul" was vexed with the filthy deeds of the Sodomites. The Holy Qur'ān thus accepts him to be what he truly was, a righteous man and a prophet who was sent to reform the Sodomites, and rejects as untrue what is related about him in the Bible, in Gen. 19:30-38. As regards Lot's wife, the Qur'ān does not accept the Bible story that she was turned into a pillar of salt for looking back when she left the Sodomites with Lot; instead, it says that she was destroyed along with the Sodomites, as she did not go with Lot (7:83, etc,), and "acted treacherously towards" him (66:10). The punishment which

113

overtook Lot's people, though often called merely a rain, is plainly stated to be a rain of stones (11:82; 15:74). In 15:73, it is called a rumbling, thus showing clearly that it was an earthquake; hence the place is said to have been "turned upside down" (15:74).

Of Abraham's sons, Isaac is accepted as a prophet by the Bible as well as the Holy Qur'ān, but a marked difference is observable about Ishmael. The Qur'ān refers to him repeatedly as one of the prophets. Nothing is said about the people to whom he was sent, but a report speaks of his having been sent to the people of Yemen. The Bible, on the other hand, does not speak of him as a prophet, but the promise made to Ishmael is not substantially different from the promise made to Abraham:

> And as for Ishmael, I have heard thee; behold I have blessed him, and will make him fruitful, and will multiply him exceedingly; twelve princes shall he beget; and I will make him a great nation (Gen. 17:20).

This shows clearly that Ishmael was righteous in the sight of God. Abraham's grandson, Jacob (11:71), is also included among the prophets; Jacob's son, Joseph, is specially mentioned, the whole of ch. 12 being devoted to his history, containing, as it does, numerous prophetical hints relative to the history of the Holy Prophet himself (12:7).

Among Abraham's descendants, and previous to Moses, is Shu'aib, who was sent to Midian, a city on the Red Sea. Shu'aib is generally considered to be the Arabic name for Jethro. He is also supposed to be the man whose daughter Moses married when he fled to Midian (28:27). He is mentioned by name only four times in the Holy Qur'ān. In his teaching special stress is laid on the giving of full measure and weight. Shu'aib is also spoken of as being sent to the dwellers of the thicket (26:176, 177), but whether or not they were the same as the people of Midian cannot be said; in all probability they were identical.

Aaron is very often mentioned with Moses and we are told that the Torah was given to them both (37:117). The chief point in which the Holy Qur'ān makes a departure from the Bible narrative is

Aaron's alleged making of a calf for the Israelites to worship (Ex. ch. 32). The Qur'ān not only clears him of idol-making, but shows him as plainly admonishing the Israelites because of their worship of the calf:

> And certainly Aaron had said to them before, O my people! you are only tried by it, and surely your Lord is the Beneficent God, therefore follow me and obey my order (20:90).

Among the prophets of the Mosaic dispensation, besides Jesus Christ, David and Solomon are given the greatest prominence, and the glory to which the Israelite kingdom arose under those prophet-kings is referred to on more than one occasion. In fact, all this is history containing prophecy of the greatness of Islam. The chapters containing it are those which were revealed at Makka when opposition to the Prophet was at its height and his cause seemed to be quite hopeless. The repetition of this history was a comfort to the Muslims as showing that the time was coming when all this opposition would be brought to naught and Islam would shine forth in all her glory. The prominence given to the history of John the Baptist and of Jesus Christ, on the one hand, and to that of David and Solomon on the other, of whom the former stood for the spiritual greatness of the Mosaic dispensation and the latter for its material greatness, was in fact a clear indication that the Holy Prophet was destined to occupy the position of both a spiritual world-teacher and a king. This is made clear by expressly calling the Prophet Muhammad the like of Moses, as has already been pointed out, and again by likening the Muhammadan dispensation to the Mosaic dispensation (24:55).

The longest notice of David is that contained in 38:17-26, which begins with his conquests and his kingdom:

> We made the mountains subject to him, to declare the glory of God at evening and sunrise, and the birds gathered together - all were obedient to him.

That his conquests and kingdom are referred to in these words is made clear by what follows: "And We strengthened his kingdom and

We gave him wisdom and a clear judgment." A similar description in 34:10 is followed by the words, "And We made iron pliant to him: make ample coats of mail," which clearly refer to wars. Notwithstanding his vast kingdom, he had to bear up with his enemies and treat them leniently:

> And has there come to thee the story of the adversaries when they made an entry into the private chamber by ascending over the walls. When they entered in upon David and he was frightened of them (38:21, 22).

Strangely enough, this account of his enemies' planning against his life has been twisted by some less careful commentators, under the influence of Jewish tradition and the Bible, into the story that David committed adultery and that two angels came to remind him of the sin. The Qur'ān plainly calls the two intruders _khaṣm_, or _enemies_, and speaks of them as finding access to his private chamber by _ascending over the walls_; thus, to suppose them to be angels is the height of absurdity. The Caliph 'Alī, when he heard the false story related about David, said: "Whoever shall relate the story of David as the story-tellers relate it, I will give him 160 stripes, and this is the punishment of those who falsely charge the prophets." This incident is related by the great commentator, Razi, who also says: "Most of the learned and those who have searched for the truth among them declare this charge to be false and condemn it as a lie and as a mischievous story."

The only other important point related about David is his slaying of Goliath (2:251) which occurs in a Madina revelation, and here, too, it is added that "God gave him kingdom and wisdom."

Not only was Solomon heir to David's kingdom (27:16), but he further widened it by conquests. Here, too, it may be mentioned that the Holy Qur'ān rejects the charge of idol-worship against Solomon, which the Bible prefers in plain words by asserting that the wives of Solomon "turned away his heart after other gods" (1 Kings 11:4). The Qur'ān disposes of this charge in a very few words:

> And Solomon did not disbelieve but the devils disbelieved (2:102).

The Rev. T.K. Cheyne shows in the *Encyclopædia Biblica* that the Bible statement is incorrect:

> That Solomon had a number of wives, both Israelite, and non-Israelite, is probable enough, but he did not make altars for all of them, nor did he himself combine the worship of his wives' gods with that of Yahwe.

The Qur'ān, however, goes further than this, for it says that the Queen of Sheba became a believer in God:

> She said, My Lord! I have been unjust to myself and I submit with Solomon to God, the Lord of the worlds (27:44).

The longest notice of Solomon is that connected with his conquest of Sheba. It starts with a description of the immense resources of his kingdom:

> O men! we have been taught the significance of the voices of birds and we have been granted of every thing; surely this is manifest grace. And his hosts of the jinn and the men and the birds were gathered to him, and they were formed into groups (27:16, 17).

The use of birds in conveying messages made birds a necessary adjunct to a military expedition, and the jinn were no doubt the hardy non-Israelite tribes subjugated to the Israelites. Elsewhere they are spoken of as "those who worked before him by the command of his Lord" (34:12), and "made for him what he pleased of fortresses and images" (34:13). Clearly these were the foreigners whom Solomon employed to build the Temple, men skilled in architecture, for the Arabs, as Tabrezi, in his commentary on Himasa, remarks, "speak of the jinn, frequently likening a man who is clever in executing affairs to the *jinni* and the *shaitan*, or the devil." Men employed by Solomon in this and similar service are elsewhere spoken of as devils:

> And the devils, every builder and diver, and others fettered in chains (38:37, 38).

These last seem to be those who were forced into service or they may have been prisoners of war.

After Solomon sets out for the conquest of Sheba, he passes the valley of the Naml, which should not be translated as the valley of the ants, for Naml, though meaning *ants*, is here used as a proper name, and *wād al-Naml*, or the valley of the Naml, is, according to the *Tāj al-'Arūs*, "situated between Jibrin and 'Asqalan." Moreover, the Namla are plainly spoken of as a tribe, in the Qāmūs which says: "Abriqa is of the waters of Namla." This tribe, which very likely intervened between Solomon and the Queen of Sheba and formed a kind of buffer state, submitted to Solomon, and hence we find Solomon giving thanks to God:

> My Lord! grant me that I should be grateful for Thy favour which Thou hast bestowed on me and on my parents. (27:19).

A similar mistake is made in connection with Hudhud, who is undoubtedly mentioned as an officer of Solomon, but the word is misunderstood to mean the *lapwing*. A similar name is Ben-hadad, a king of Syria (1 Kings 20:1), and the Arab writers speak of a king of Himyar as Hudad. The mistake arises from the fact that his name is mentioned in connection with the review of birds (27:20); but the reason for this mention seems to be that the man so named was an officer of the Intelligence department of Solomon's army. All that is related of him in the ten verses that follow clearly shows him to be a man and not a bird, for he brings to Solomon news about the Queen of Sheba, whom he finds along with her people "adoring the sun instead of God" (27:24) and doing many unrighteous things: "And the devil has made their deeds fair-seeming to them and thus turned them from the way." Only a man could judge what a false belief or a wicked deed was; it is beyond the ken of a bird.

The Queen of Sheba at first sends to Solomon a present which he considers as an affront and he threatens to attack her territory. She submits to Solomon and comes to him, and is asked to "enter the palace" which means that she became his wife. In the palace, water ran under glass, which the queen mistook for water itself. Thus did Solomon make her realize her error in worshipping the sun which was only an outward object, while the real source of life and power was God, Whose hand, unseen by man, worked in such objects. It is then that the queen believes in God and gives up the worship of visible objects.

Solomon is again mentioned in connection with the destruction of the city of Saba, or Sheba, in ch. 34. Here we are told that the wind was made subservient to Solomon "which made a month's journey in the morning and a month's journey in the evening" (34:12). In 21:81 the words are:

> And We made subservient to Solomon the wind blowing violent, pursuing its course by His command to the land which We had blessed.

The reference in both places is to Solomon's fleet which ran between the gulf of Aqaba and Ophir on the eastern coast of the Arabian peninsula, and brought him "fabulous amounts of gold and tropical products," according to the *Jewish Encyclopædia*, giving him, "unlimited means for increasing the glory of his capital, city and palace." This is referred to in what follows, in 34:12 and 13, the making to flow of "a fountain of molten brass" and the making of "fortresses and images and bowls … and cooking pots." Yet, with all this glory, Solomon's death was also the death-knell of his kingdom, and his successor was only "a creature of the earth that ate away his staff," the reference being to the life of ease and luxury which Rehoboam led, the eating away of the staff indicating the disruption of his kingdom. Elsewhere we are told that Solomon's heir was "a mere body" (38:34), and that, when Solomon saw this, "he turned to God" and prayed for a kingdom which should not be in danger of being wasted by others — the spiritual kingdom. We are also told that Solomon had at heart no attraction towards the wealth and the good things of this life. "I love the good things on account of the remembrance of my Lord" (38:32), he said, when a number of well-bred and swift horses were brought to him.

Of the other Biblical prophets, Job is mentioned four times, the longest notice of him being 38:41-44, which is very probably an account of his flight from one place to another, for, when he complains of toil and torment, he is urged to go on further — a lesson not to despair under difficulties. He is also spoken of as being given "his family and the like of them with them," which signifies that he was brought back to his family and was blessed with more children. A similar statement occurs in 21:83, 84. The forty-two chapters of the Bible are here condensed into perhaps as many words, and with more effect: "We found him patient; most excellent the servant, for he was frequent in returning to God."

References to Jonah are more frequent and he is mentioned in one of the earliest revelations, where the Holy Prophet is told to bear persecution patiently and not to be like Jonah, who is called "the companion of the fish" (68:48-50). The whole is explained in another early revelation (37:139-148), probably later than that referred to above. Jonah flies from his people, and 68:48 shows that he fled before he received the Divine commandment to fly. He comes to a boat and is cast into the river. A fish draws him into his mouth. The word used by the Holy Qur'ān does not necessarily mean *devoured*. There is no mention of his remaining in the belly of the fish for three days and three nights, all that is said being: "But had it not been that he was one of those who glorify Us, he would have tarried in its belly to the day they are raised" (37:143, 144), *i.e.*, he would have been devoured and would have met death in its belly. Apparently, therefore, he was not devoured by the fish. He was saved and sent to a hundred thousand people (37:147). In 10:98 we are told that the people of Jonah believed in him and profited by their faith.

John the Baptist and his father, Zacharias, are mentioned twice at considerable length (19:1-15 and 3:38-41), and both these accounts are followed by an account of the birth of Jesus Christ. When Zacharias receives the news of the birth of a son, he wonders and is assured in words similar to those in which Mary wonders and is assured; but Zacharias is not struck dumb, as in Luke 1:20, and there is no mention of unbelief on his part. On the other hand, as if to contradict Luke, it is related that he was ordered not to speak to people for three days, being otherwise in sound health (19:10), and the object of this silence is also made clear:

> And remember thy Lord much and glorify Him in the
> evening and in the morning (3:41).

It may be added that in the Holy Qur'ān Zacharias is expressly spoken of as a prophet, in 6:85, and that John was a prophet is mentioned more than once (6:85; 3:39; 19:12). In the Bible, however, the Old Testament is brought to an end with Malachi, while the "New Dispensation" cannot admit of a prophet other than Jesus. Strangely enough, however, John is pronounced to be a prophet — nay, "more than a prophet" — by Jesus Christ himself (Matt. 11:9), and thus the position is quite anomalous. Further, the angel Gabriel who brought revelation to prophets is spoken of as bringing revelation to Zacharias (Luke 1:19). In fact, the anomaly is due to the supposition of a break in prophethood previous to the advent of Jesus, where actually there is none, as Jesus was only part of the chain of prophethood that extends from Moses to Jesus, the last link no doubt, as Moses was the first.

John the Baptist is, however, declared by the Gospel-writers to be greater than even Jesus Christ. He was "filled with the Holy Ghost, even from his mother's womb" (Luke 1:15), while the Holy Ghost did not descend upon Jesus until he was baptized by John (Matt. 3:16). Jesus says that, "among them that are born of women, there hath not risen a greater than John the Baptist" (Matt. 11:11), and Jesus himself was undoubtedly born of a woman. Even the Holy Qur'ān speaks of him in terms of great praise:

> We granted him wisdom while yet a child and tenderness from Us and purity, and he was one who guarded against evil ... and he was not insolent, disobedient (19:12-14).

This shows clearly that, according to the Holy Qur'ān, John was pure and sinless and never disobeyed God. It is not meant that other prophets were not as pure; in fact, what is said of one prophet is equally true of others.

Elias is mentioned twice, once at some length, showing that he preached against the worship of Bal or the sun-god (37:123-132). Elisha is mentioned once only by name (6:86) along with Ishmael and Jonah and Lot — all four being stated as excelling the world. Dhul-kifl (21:85) is probably Ezekiel. Joshua is not mentioned by name, but is referred to along with Caleb, in 5:23. The prophet

Samuel is also not mentioned by name, but is referred to in 2:246-248. Daniel's vision (Dan. 8:3) is referred to in 18:83, and Ezekiel's vision is referred to in 2:259.

Chapter 4

Some Misconceptions About Quranic Teachings

Section 1
Tolerance

There is very general and very deep-rooted misconception that the Qur'ān preaches intolerance, and that Muhammad preached his faith with the sword in one hand and the Qur'ān in the other. Misrepresentation could go no further. The basic principle of Islam, a faith in all the prophets of the world, is enough to give the lie to this allegation. The great and liberal mind that preached not only love and respect for the founders of the great religions of the world but much more than that — *faith in them* — could not shrink to the narrowness of intolerance for those very religions. Tolerance is not in fact the word that can sufficiently indicate the breadth of the attitude of Islam towards other religions. It preaches equal love for all, equal respect for all, and equal faith in all.

Again, intolerance could not be ascribed to a book which altogether excludes compulsion from the sphere of religion. "There is no compulsion in religion" (2:256), it lays down in the clearest words. In fact, the Holy Qur'ān is full of statements showing that belief in this or that religion is a person's own concern, and that he is given the choice of adopting one way or another: that, if he accepts truth, it is for his own good, and that, if he sticks to error, it is to his own detriment. I give below a few of these quotations:

> We have shown him the way, he may be thankful or unthankful (76:3).

> The truth is from your Lord, so let him who wishes believe and let him who wishes disbelieve (18:29).

> Indeed there have come to you clear proofs from your Lord: whoever will therefore see, it is for the good of his own soul, and whoever will disbelieve, it shall be against him (6:104).

> If you do good, you will do good for your own souls; and if you do evil, it shall be for them (17:7).

The Muslims were allowed to fight indeed, but what was the object? Not to compel the unbelievers to accept Islam, for it was against all the broad principles upon which they had hitherto been brought up. No, it was to establish religious freedom, to stop all religious persecution, to protect the houses of worship of all religions, mosques among them. Here are a few quotations:

> And had there not been God's repelling some people by others, there would have been pulled down cloisters and churches and synagogues and mosques in which God's name is much remembered (22:40).

> And fight against them until there is no more persecution, and religion is only for God (2:193).

> And fight against them until there is no more persecution, and all religions should be for God (8:39).

Under what conditions was the permission to fight given to the Muslims? Every student of Islamic history knows that the Holy Prophet and his companions were subjected to the severest persecutions, as Islam began to gain ground at Makka; over a hundred of them fled to Abyssinia, but persecutions grew still more relentless. Ultimately, the Muslims had to take refuge in Madina, but they were not left alone even there, and the sword was taken up by the enemy to annihilate Islam and the Muslims. The Qur'ān bears express testimony to this:

> Permission to fight is given to those upon whom war is made because they are oppressed, and God is well able to assist them; those who have been expelled from their homes

without a just cause except that they say, Our Lord is God (22:39, 40).

Later, the express condition was laid down:

> And fight in the way of God against those who fight against you, and do not exceed, for God does not love those who exceed the limits (2:190).

The Qur'ān, therefore, allowed fighting only to save a persecuted community from powerful oppressors, and hence the condition was laid down that fighting was to be stopped as soon as persecution ceased:

> But if they desist, then God is Forgiving, Merciful. And fight against them until there is no more persecution (2:192, 193).

If the enemy offered peace, peace was to be accepted, though the enemy's intention might be only to deceive the Muslims:

> And if they incline to peace, do thou incline to it and trust in God; He is the Hearing, the Knowing. And if they intend to deceive thee, then surely God is sufficient for thee (8:61, 62).

The Prophet made treaties of peace with his enemies; one such treaty brought about the famous truce of Hudaibiya, the terms of which were not only disadvantageous, but also humiliating to the Muslims. According to the terms of this treaty, "if an unbeliever, being converted to Islam, went over to the Muslims, he was to be returned, but if a Muslim went over to the unbeliever, he was not to be given back to the Muslims." This clause of the treaty cuts at the root of all allegations of the use of force by the Holy Prophet. It also shows the strong conviction of the Holy Prophet that neither would Muslims go back to unbelief, nor would the new converts to Islam be deterred from embracing Islam because the Prophet gave them no shelter. And these expectations proved true, for while not a single Muslim deserted Islam, a large number came over to Islam, and, being refused shelter at Madina, formed a colony of their own in neutral territory.

It is a mistake to suppose that the conditions related above were abrogated at any time. The condition to fight "against those who fight against you" remained in force to the last. The last expedition led by the Holy Prophet was the famous Tabuk expedition, and every historian of Islam knows that, though the Prophet had marched a very long distance to Tabuk at the head of an army of thirty thousand, yet, when he found that the enemy did not fulfil the condition laid down above, he returned, and did not allow his troops to attack the enemy territory. Nor is there a single direction in the latest revelation on this subject, in ch. 9, the Immunity, that goes against this condition. The opening verse of that chapter speaks expressly of "idolaters with whom you made an agreement," and then, v. 4, excepts from its purview "those of the idolaters with whom you made an agreement, then they have not failed you in anything and have not backed up any one against you," thus showing clearly that the "immunity" related only to such idolatrous tribes as had first made agreements with the Muslims and then, violating them, killed and persecuted the Muslims wherever they found them, as v. 10 says expressly:

> They do not pay regard to ties of relationship nor to those of covenant in the case of a believer.

Such people are also spoken of in an earlier revelation:

> Those with whom thou makest an agreement, then they break their agreement every time and they are not careful of their duty (8:56).

Further on, in ch. 9, the condition of the enemy attacking the Muslims first is plainly repeated:

> What! will you not fight a people who broke their oaths and aimed at the expulsion of the Apostle, and they attacked you first? (9:13).

So from first to last, the Holy Qur'ān allowed fighting only against those who fought Muslims first; it allowed expressly only fighting in defense without which the Muslims could not live, and it clearly forbade aggressive war. The waging of war on unbelievers to compel them to accept Islam is a myth pure and simple, a thing unknown to the Holy Qur'ān. It was the enemy that waged war on the Muslims to turn them away from their religion, as the Holy Book so clearly asserts:

> And they will not cease fighting against you until they turn you back from your religion, if they can (2:217).

It is sometimes asserted that the Qur'ān forbids relations of friendship with the followers of other religions. How could a book which allows a man to have his comrade in life a woman following another religion (5:5), say in the same breath that no friendly relations can be had with the followers of other religions? The loving relation of husband and wife is the friendliest of all relations and, when this is expressly permitted, there is not the least reason to suppose that other friendly relations are forbidden. The fact is that, wherever there is a prohibition against making friends with other people, it relates only to the people who were at war with the Muslims, and this is plainly stated in the Qur'ān:

> God does not forbid you respecting those who have not made war against you on account of your religion, and have not driven you forth from your homes, that you show them kindness and deal with them justly; for God loves the doers of justice. God forbids you respecting only those who made war upon you on account of your religion, and drove you forth from your homes and backed up others in your expulsion, that you should not make friends with them, and whoever makes friends with them, these are the unjust (60:8, 9).

Another widely prevailing misconception may also be noted here. It is generally thought that the Qur'ān provides a death sentence for those who desert the religion of Islam. Anyone who takes the trouble to read the Qur'ān will see that there is not the least ground for such a supposition. The Qur'ān speaks repeatedly of people going back to unbelief after believing, but never once does it say that they should be killed or punished. I give here a few quotations:

And whoever of you turns back from his religion, then he dies while an unbeliever — these it is whose deeds shall go for nothing in this world and the hereafter (2:217).

O you who believe! should one of you turn back from his religion, then God will bring a people whom He shall love and they too shall love Him (5:54).

Those who disbelieve after their believing, then increase in disbelief, their repentance shall not be accepted, and these are they that go astray (3:90).

On the other hand, the Qur'ān speaks of a plan of the Jews to adopt Islam first and then desert it, thus creating the impression that Islam was not a religion worth having (3:72). Such a scheme could never have entered their heads while living at Madina where the government was Muslim, if apostacy, according to the Qurānic law, were punishable with death. The misconception seems to have arisen from the fact that people who, after becoming apostates, joined the enemy, were treated as enemies, or that, where an apostate took the life of a Muslim, he was put to death, not for changing his religion, but for committing murder.

Section 2

The Position of Woman

The belief that according to the Qur'ān woman has no soul is almost general in the West. Probably it took hold of the mind of Europe at a time when Europeans had no access to the Qur'ān. No other religious book and no other reformer has done one-tenth of what the Holy Qur'ān or the Holy Prophet Muhammad has done to raise the position of woman. Read the Qur'ān and you find good and righteous women being given the same position as good and righteous men. Both sexes are spoken of in the same terms. The highest favour which God has bestowed upon man is the gift of Divine revelation, and we find women, to whom Divine revelation came, spoken of along with men:

> And We revealed to Moses' mother, saying Give him suck, then when thou fearest for him, cast him into the river and do not fear nor grieve, for We will bring him back to thee and make him one of the apostles (28:7).
>
> When We revealed to thy mother what was revealed (20:38).
>
> And when the angels said, O Mary! God has chosen thee and purified thee and chosen thee above the women of the world (3:42).

Further, where the Holy Qur'ān speaks of the great prophets of God, saying: "And mention Abraham in the Book" (19:41), "And mention Moses in the Book" (19:51), and so on, it speaks of a woman in exactly the same terms: "And mention Mary in the Book" (19:16). No other religious book has given such a high spiritual position to a woman.

The Qur'ān makes no difference between man and woman in the bestowal of reward for the good he or she does:

> I will not waste the work of a worker among you, whether male or female, the one of you being from the other (3:195).

> And whoever does good deeds, whether male or female, and he is a believer — these shall enter the garden, and they shall not be dealt with a jot unjustly (4:124).

> Whoever does good, whether male or female, and he is a believer, We will certainly make him live a happy life, and We will certainly give them their reward for the best of what they did (16:97).

> And whoever does good, whether male or female, and he is a believer, these shall enter the garden, in which they shall be given sustenance without measure (40:40).

Also, 33:35, speaking of good women alongside of good men, enumerates every good quality as being possessed by women exactly as it is possessed by men, and ends with the words, "God has prepared for them forgiveness and a mighty reward." With God, therefore, according to the Qur'ān, there is no difference between men and women, and morally and spiritually they can rise to the same eminence.

On the material side, too, we find no difference, except what nature requires for its own ends. A woman can earn, inherit and own property and dispose of it just as a man can, and the Holy Qur'ān is explicit on all these points:

> Men shall have the benefit of what they earn and women shall have the benefit of what they earn (4:32).

> Men shall have a portion of what the parents and the near relatives leave, and women shall have a portion of what the parents and the near relatives leave (4:7).

> But if they (the women) of themselves be pleased to give up to you a portion of dowry, then eat it with enjoyment and with wholesome result (4:4).

Woman, in Arabia, had no rights of property nay, she herself was part of the inheritance, and was taken possession of along with other property. She had no right to the property of her deceased husband or father. The Qur'ān took her from this low position and raised her to a position of perfect freedom as regards her property rights and her right to inheritance, a position which, among other nations, she has only partly attained and that after centuries of hard struggle.

It is, however, asserted that polygamy and *pardah* (seclusion), as enjoined in the Holy Qur'ān, have done more harm to woman than the benefit conferred on her by bestowal of property rights. The fact is that a great misunderstanding exists on these two points. Monogamy is the rule in Islam and polygamy only an exception allowed subject to certain conditions. The following two verses are the only authority for the sanction of polygamy, and let us see how far they carry us:

> And if you fear that you cannot act equitably towards orphans, marry such women as seem good to you, two and three and four; but if you fear that you will not do justice between them, then marry only one or what your right hands possess; this is more proper that you may not deviate from the right course (4:3).

> And they ask thee a decision about women. Say, God makes known to you His decision concerning them, and that which is recited to you in the Book concerning orphans of the women to whom you do not give what is appointed for them while you are disinclined to marry them (4:127).

Now the first of these verses allows polygamy on the express condition that "you cannot act equitably towards orphans," and what is meant is made clear by the second verse, which contains a clear reference to the first verse in the words, "that which is recited to you in the Book concerning orphans of women." The Arabs were guilty of a double injustice to widows; they did not give them and their children a share in the inheritance of their husbands, nor were they inclined to marry widows who had children, because the responsibility for the maintenance of the children would in that case devolve upon them. The Qur'ān remedied both these evils; it gave a share of inheritance to the widow with a share also for the orphans, and it commended the taking of such widows in marriage, and allowed polygamy expressly for this purpose. It should, therefore, be clearly understood that monogamy is the rule in Islam and polygamy is allowed only as a remedial measure, and that, not for the sake of the man, but for the sake of the widow and her children. This permission was given at a time when the wars, which were forced on the Muslims, had decimated the men, so that many widows and orphans were left for whom it was necessary to provide. A provision was made in the form of polygamy so that the widow should find a home and a protector and the orphans should have paternal care and affection. Europe to-day has its problem of the excess of women, and let it consider if it can solve that problem otherwise than by sanctioning a limited polygamy. Perhaps the only other way is prostitution, which prevails widely in all European countries and, where the law of the country does not recognize it, it is recognized in practice. Nature will have its course, and allowing illicit intercourse is the only other alternative to a limited polygamy.

As regards the seclusion of women, the Qur'ān never prohibited women from going out of their houses for their needs. In the time of the Prophet, women went regularly to mosques, and said their prayers along with men, standing in a separate row. They also joined their husbands in the labour of the field; they even went with the army to the field of battle, and looked after the wounded, removing them from the field if necessary, and helped fighting men in many other ways. They could even fight the enemy in an emergency. No occupation was prohibited to them, and they could do any work they chose. The only restrictions on their liberty are contained in the following verses:

> Say to the believing men that they cast down their looks and guard their private parts; that is purer for them; God is aware of what they do. Say to the believing women that they cast down their looks, and guard their private parts and not display their ornaments except what appears thereof; and let them wear their head-coverings over their bosoms (24:30, 31).

Now the real restriction contained in these verses is that both men and women should, when they meet each other, cast down their looks, but there is an additional restriction in the case of women that *they should not display their ornaments* with the exception of "what appears thereof." The exception has been explained as meaning "what is customary and natural to uncover." That women went to mosques with their faces uncovered is recognized on all hands, and there is also a saying of the Holy Prophet that, when a woman reaches the age of puberty, she should cover her body *except the face and the hands*. The majority of the commentators are also of opinion that the exception relates to the face and the hands. Hence, while a display of beauty is forbidden, the restriction does not interfere with the necessary activities of women. She can do any work that she likes to earn her livlihood, for the Holy Qur'ān says plainly, as already quoted, that women shall have the benefit of *what they earn*. A limited seclusion and a limited polygamy do not, therefore, interfere with the necessary activities of woman; they are both meant for her protection and as preventives against the loose sexual relations which ultimately undermine society.

Books on Islam

World-renowned literature produced by
The Ahmadiyya Anjuman Ishā'at Islam, Lahore (Pakistan)

"Probably no man living has done longer or more valuable service for the cause of Islamic revival than Maulana Muhammad Ali of Lahore. His literary works, with those of the late Khwaja Kamal-ud-Din, have given fame and distinction to the Ahmadiyya Movement" —
M. Pickthall, famous British Muslim and translator of Holy Quran.

Books by Maulana Muhammad Ali:

The Holy Qur'ān   Pp. lxxvi + 1256

Arabic text, with English translation, exhaustive commentary, comprehensive Introduction, and large Index. Leading English translation. Has since 1917 influenced millions of people all over the world. Model for all later translations. Thoroughly revised in 1951.

"To deny the excellence of Muhammad Ali's translation, the influence it has exercised, and its proselytising utility, would be to deny the light of the sun" — Maulana Abdul Majid Daryabadi, leader of orthodox Muslim opinion in India.

"The first work published by any Muslim with the thoroughness worthy of Quranic scholarship and achieving the standards of modern publications" — Amir Ali in *The Student's Quran*, London, 1961.

The Religion of Islam

Comprehensive and monumental work on the sources, principles, and practices of Islam. First published 1936.

". . . an extremely useful work, almost indispensable to the students of Islam" — Dr Sir Muhammad Iqbal, renowned Muslim philosopher.

"Such a book is greatly needed when in many Muslim countries we see persons eager for the revival of Islam, making mistakes through lack of just this knowledge" — 'Islamic Culture', October 1936.

A Manual of Hadith   Pp. 400

Sayings of Holy Prophet Muhammad on practical life of a Muslim, classified by subject. Arabic text, English translation and explanatory notes.

Muhammad The Prophet

Researched biography of Holy Prophet, sifting authentic details from spurious reports. Corrects many misconceptions regarding Holy Prophet's life.

Early Caliphate   pp. 214

History of Islam under first four Caliphs.

"(1) Muhammad The Prophet, (2) The Early Caliphate, by Muhammad Ali together constitute the most complete and satisfactory history of the early Muslims hitherto compiled in English" — 'Islamic Culture', April 1935.

Living Thoughts of Prophet Muhammad   Pp. 150

Life of Holy Prophet, and his teachings on various subjects.

The New World Order   Pp. 170

Islam's solution to major modern world problems.

Founder of the Ahmadiyya Movement *1984 U.S.A. edition,* Pp. 100.

Biography of Hazrat Mirza by Maulana Muhammad Ali who worked closely with
him for the last eight years of the Founder's life.

Other major publications:

The Teachings of Islam by Hazrat Mirza Ghulam Ahmad. Pp. 226

Brilliant, much-acclaimed exposition of the Islamic path for the physical, moral and
spiritual progress of man, first given as a lecture in 1896.

*". . . the best and most attractive presentation of the faith of Muhammad which we
have yet come across"* — 'Theosophical Book Notes'.

*Other English translations as well as original Urdu books of Hazrat Mirza are
also available.*

Muhammad in World Scriptures by Maulana Abdul Haque Vidyarthi.
Pp. 1500 in 3 vols.

Unique research by scholar of religious scriptures and languages, showing
prophecies about the Holy Prophet Muhammad in all major world scriptures.

Ahmadiyyat in the Service of Islam, by Naseer A. Faruqui, ex-Head of
the Pakistan Civil Service. Pp. 149, printed in the U.S.A.

1983 book dealing with the beliefs, claims and achievements of Hazrat Mirza
Ghulam Ahmad, and the work of the Lahore Ahmadiyya Movement.

The Great Religions of the World, by Mrs U. Samad. Pp. 258
Anecdotes from the Life of the Prophet Muhammad, by Mumtaz A.
Faruqui. Pp. 102
Anecdotes from the Life of the Promised Messiah, by Mumtaz A.
Faruqui. Pp. 131

Islam & Christianity by Naseer A. Faruqui

For prices and delivery of these books and inquiries about other books and free literature,
please contact:

Ahmadiyya Anjuman Ishaat Islam (Lahore) U.S.A.
P.O. Box 3370, Dublin, OH 43016-0176, U.S.A.

Email : aaii@aol.com
Phone : (614) 873-1030   Fax : (614) 873-1022
Website : www.muslim.org